The MAILBOX Day-by-Day Kindergarten PLANS

grade

D1371128

A Week's Worth of Ideas for Each of 40 Popular Themes

- Colors
- Apples
- All About Me
- Pumpkins
- Family
- Fall Harvest

- Bears
- Happy Holidays
- Snow and Mittens
- 100th Day
- Space
- Weather

- The Farm
- Flowers
- Caterpillars and Butterflies
- Pond Life
- Ocean
- ...and many more!

Plans for the whole year!

Editorial Team: Becky S. Andrews, Diane Badden, Kimberley Bruck, Karen A. Brudnak, Kitty Campbell, Jenny Chapman, Pam Crane, Lynette Dickerson, Lynn Drolet, Amy Erickson, Sue Fleischmann, Sarah Foreman, Ada Goren, Deborah Garmon, Karen Grossman, Tazmen Hansen, Marsha Heim, Lori Z. Henry, Lucia Kemp Henry, Amy Kirtley-Hill, Debra Liverman, Kimberly Brugger-Murphy, Sharon Murphy, Jennifer Nunn, Tina Petersen, Mark Rainey, Greg D. Rieves, Kelly Robertson, Hope Rodgers, Leanne Stratton Swinson, Rachael Traylor, Zane Williard

www.themailbox.com

©2009 The Mailbox® Books
All rights reserved.
ISBN10 #1-56234-880-9 • ISBN13 #978-1-56234-880-9

Manufactured in the United States
10 9 8 7 6 5 4 3 2 1

Table of

40 Weekly Themes

Contents

What's Inside

Centers →

Each theme includes:

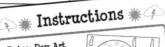

Day-by-Day Activities →

Timesavers →

Plus...

Online Extras at → **themailboxbooks.com** →

- **Patterns**
- **Full-color picture cards**
- **...and more!**

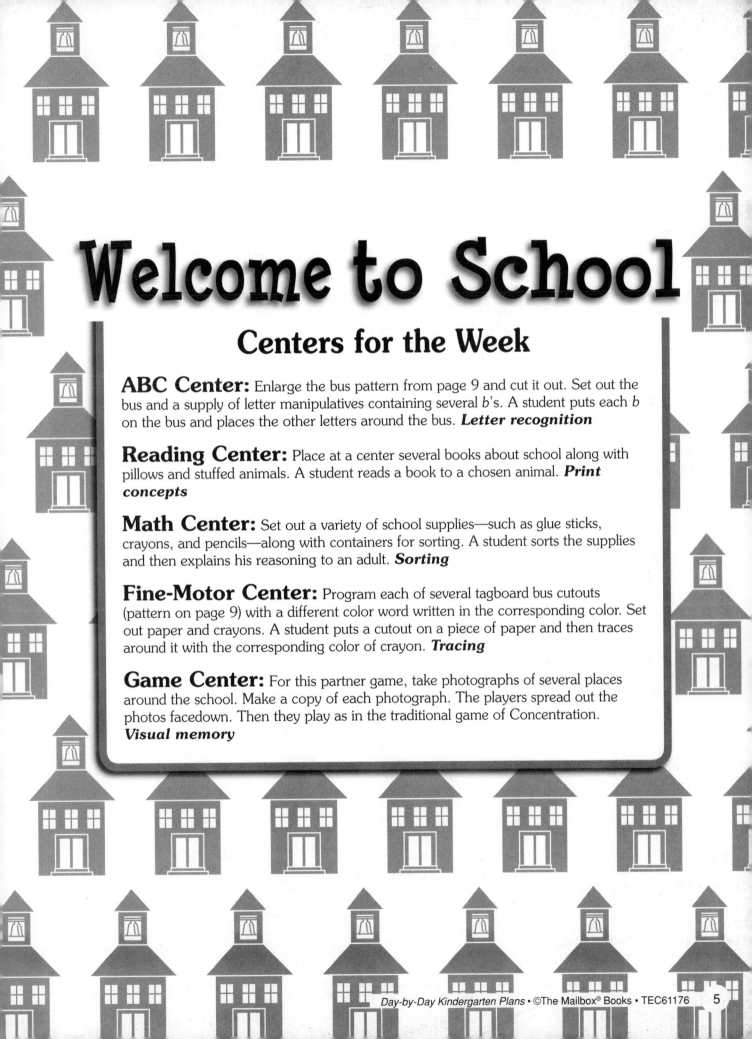

Welcome to School

Centers for the Week

ABC Center: Enlarge the bus pattern from page 9 and cut it out. Set out the bus and a supply of letter manipulatives containing several *b*'s. A student puts each *b* on the bus and places the other letters around the bus. ***Letter recognition***

Reading Center: Place at a center several books about school along with pillows and stuffed animals. A student reads a book to a chosen animal. ***Print concepts***

Math Center: Set out a variety of school supplies—such as glue sticks, crayons, and pencils—along with containers for sorting. A student sorts the supplies and then explains his reasoning to an adult. ***Sorting***

Fine-Motor Center: Program each of several tagboard bus cutouts (pattern on page 9) with a different color word written in the corresponding color. Set out paper and crayons. A student puts a cutout on a piece of paper and then traces around it with the corresponding color of crayon. ***Tracing***

Game Center: For this partner game, take photographs of several places around the school. Make a copy of each photograph. The players spread out the photos facedown. Then they play as in the traditional game of Concentration. ***Visual memory***

Morning Group Time	Read-Alouds and Art

Monday

Take your students on a tour of the school. Then give each student a sheet of paper and have her draw a place the class visited. Invite her to dictate a relevant sentence; then write it on her paper. **Written expression**

We saw the library.

Invite students to name worries children may have about school. Record their thoughts on the board. Then read aloud *Wemberly Worried* by Kevin Henkes. At the end of the story, have students compare the listed worries with Wemberly's worries. **Prior knowledge**

Tuesday

Sit in a circle with students. To begin, roll a beach ball to a student. Then have him say and complete a simple sentence, such as "My name is _____." Next, ask him to roll the ball to a classmate, and have that youngster take a turn in the same manner. Continue as described until each student has had a turn. **Oral language**

Revisit the page in yesterday's book where Wemberly meets Jewel. Review how the girls become friends. Then guide students to brainstorm a list of ways they can make friends. **Connecting literature to experience**

Wednesday

Designate a different area of the room for each type of transportation students use to come to school. Instruct each student to stand in the area that corresponds with how she gets to school. Once each student is in place, have students compare the number of children in each group. **Comparing sets**

Show students the cover of *Annabelle Swift, Kindergartner* by Amy Schwartz and point out Annabelle. Ask students to tell how they think Annabelle feels and invite them to share their reasoning. Then encourage students to check their ideas as you read the book aloud. **Prior knowledge**

Thursday

Place in a backpack a variety of school supplies, such as a box of crayons, a pair of scissors, a pencil, and a bottle of glue. Show the items to students and then return them to the backpack. Ask a student to name from memory an item in the backpack. Then remove the named item from the backpack. Continue in this manner until the backpack is empty. **Visual memory**

Bring in a small snack for each student. Revisit the page in yesterday's story where Annabelle counts the milk money. Then give each student several imitation pennies. Have her count out five pennies to "purchase" a snack from you. **Counting**

Friday

Give each student a large paper circle. Have him illustrate it to show something he wants to learn during the year. Then ask him to dictate a caption for you to write. After students share their goals, make a caterpillar by posting the circles in a line behind a caterpillar head cutout. **Setting goals**

A Day at School
(See directions on page 8.)

Literacy and Math

Give each student a copy of the bus pattern and passenger cards from page 9. Write a number from 1 to 8 on the board and have students identify it. Then instruct each student to place the corresponding number of passengers on his bus. Continue as described with different numbers. **Number recognition, counting**

Copy the school tool patterns from page 9 and then cut them out so there is one for each child. Program each cutout with an uppercase letter, writing each letter on exactly two cutouts. Give each student a cutout. Have each child find the student with the same letter. Then ask the students in each pair to write their letter on the board and identify it. **Matching letters**

Have students name things they do in the morning to get ready for school. Then instruct each youngster to complete "Getting Ready for School." (See directions on page 8.) **Sequencing**

Show students a variety of school tools along with other objects such as kitchen utensils. Lay two plastic hoops on the floor and designate one hoop for school tools and one hoop for items that are not school tools. Help students sort the items into the appropriate hoops. **Sorting**

Stack a set of student name cards facedown. Silently hold up the first card and have the corresponding student stand up as soon as she recognizes her name. Once she stands, hold up the next card. Continue as described until each student is standing. Play again, encouraging students to shorten the time it takes. **Name recognition**

Song

(sung to the tune of "The Farmer in the Dell")

I love to go to school!
I love to go to school!
It's where we play, laugh, and learn.
I love to go to school!

Print concepts: Display the song on chart paper. After students are familiar with the lyrics, guide them to find all the two-letter words.

Journal Prompts

- Draw yourself on the first day of school. Write about the day.

- Draw your favorite thing to count. Write and complete the following sentence: "I can count to _____."

- Draw yourself on the playground. Write and complete the following sentence: "I like to play _____."

- Draw an activity you do at school. Write about it.

- Draw your teacher. Write about him or her.

Instructions

A Day at School

Materials for one project: adhesive label with your school name, 12" x 18" construction paper prefolded as shown, construction paper scraps, crayons, markers, scissors, glue, and additional materials for illustrating the school, such as small rectangular sponges and tempera paints for painting bricks and shingles

Steps:
1. Cut off the top corners of your paper to make a roof.
2. Unfold your paper and draw several school activities you enjoy. Label them if desired.
3. Refold your paper. Decorate the front of it to look like your school.
4. Attach the label to the school.

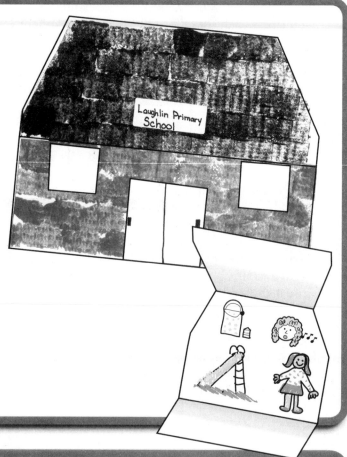

Getting Ready for School

Materials for one activity: copy of page 10, sentence strip, scissors, glue

Steps:
1. Cut apart the picture cards.
2. Choose the pictures that show what you do to get ready for school.
3. Glue the pictures on the sentence strip in the order in which you do the activities each morning.

Bus Pattern
Use with the "Welcome to School" unit on pages 5–8.

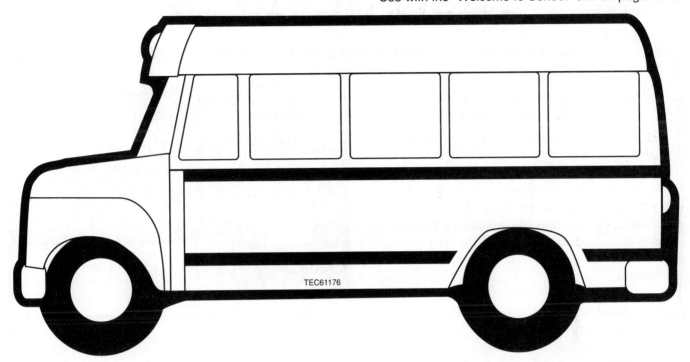

TEC61176

Passenger Cards
Use with the "Welcome to School" unit on pages 5–8.

TEC61176   TEC61176   TEC61176   TEC61176   TEC61176   TEC61176   TEC61176   TEC61176

School Tool Patterns
Use with the "Welcome to School" unit on pages 5–8.

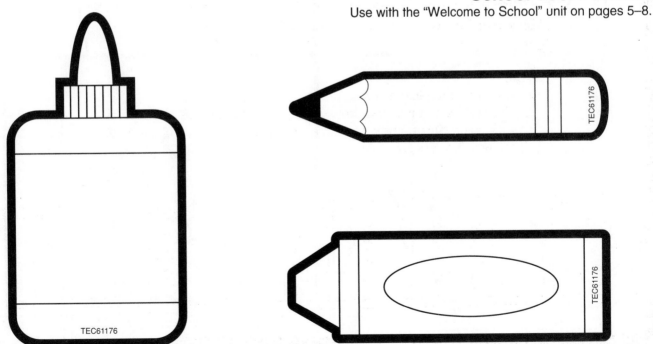

TEC61176

Picture Cards

Use with the "Welcome to School" unit on pages 5–8.

TEC61176

TEC61176

TEC61176

TEC61176

TEC61176

TEC61176

Colors

Centers for the Week

Reading Center: Write the eight basic color words in the corresponding colors on separate cards. Set out a supply of crayons. A student places each crayon on the matching card. ***Word recognition***

Writing Center: Write a different color word on each of several sentence strips with markers of the corresponding colors. Laminate the strips and set out a supply of wipe-off markers. A student traces the word on each strip and then writes the word on the blank part of the strip. ***Tracing, writing***

Math Center: Set out a supply of colored pom-poms and a muffin tin. A student sorts the pom-poms by color, putting the pom-poms of each color in a separate section of the tin. ***Sorting***

Fine-Motor Center: Hide several different-colored objects of various colors in a plastic tub containing packing peanuts. Gather one sheet of paper of each color and label it with the corresponding number of objects. A student uses tongs to remove each object and put it on the appropriate paper. When the number of objects on a paper matches the corresponding number, she knows she has found all the objects of that color. ***Hand-eye coordination***

Game Center: For this partner game, make two construction paper squares of each of several colors. Back each square with a slightly larger white card. One player mixes up the cards and spreads them out facedown. Then the players play as in the traditional game of Concentration. ***Visual memory***

Morning Group Time	Read-Alouds and Art
Monday Post around the room several large signs, each with a different color word written in the corresponding color. Announce a color. Then have each student wearing clothing with the designated color go to the corresponding sign. Continue as described with the remaining color words. **Word recognition**	Show students the front cover of *My Crayons Talk* by Patricia Hubbard and read the title aloud. Encourage students to imagine that crayons can talk and invite them to tell what they think crayons would talk about. Encourage students to check their ideas as you read the book aloud. **Prior knowledge**
Tuesday Gather a class supply of crayons, varying the quantity of each color. Give each student a crayon. Then instruct him to find classmates who have the same color as he does and have them stand together in a designated area. When each youngster is in the appropriate area, guide students to compare the groups using words such as *more, fewer, equal, most,* and *least.* **Comparing sets**	Revisit yesterday's story. Then have each student complete a page for a class book. (See directions on page 14.) **Written expression** 
Wednesday Place colorful blank cards in a bag and have students sit in a circle. In turn, each student takes a card at random. She holds it up and then uses a complete sentence to name an object of the same color. **Oral language** *The sun is yellow.*	Read aloud *Little Blue and Little Yellow* by Leo Lionni. Then display an enlarged copy of the person pattern on page 27 that you have labeled "Friend." Invite students to name qualities of a good friend and record the corresponding words on the cutout. **Story theme**
Thursday Give each student several shape cutouts of various colors and have him spread out the cutouts in front of him. Announce a shape of a certain color. Then ask any student with a matching cutout to stand up and hold it above his head. Continue as described with different-colored shapes. **Shape and color recognition**	Revisit the page in yesterday's story where Little Blue and Little Yellow hug. Set out several clear cups of water. Put a few drops of blue food coloring in one cup. Add a few drops of yellow food coloring and stir. After observing what happens, mix other colors in the remaining cups, pausing for students to predict what colors will result. **Mixing colors**
Friday Place a class supply of crayons in a basket. Invite each student to choose a crayon and then walk to an object of the same color. After every student is near an object, have each youngster name her object and its color. **Color identification**	**Swirls of Color** *(See directions on page 14.)* 

Literacy and Math

✓ Divide the class into groups. Give each group a small paper bag containing Unifix cubes of two different colors. (Vary the quantities in the bags.) Instruct each group to make towers of like-colored cubes and compare the heights of the towers. Then have the class compare the heights of all the like-colored towers. **Comparing heights**

✓ Write on each of several different-colored cards the corresponding color word. Puzzle-cut the cards between the letters. Give each student a piece at random. Instruct him to find classmates with like-colored pieces. After students assemble the puzzles, have each group read and spell its color word. **Spelling**

✓ Give each student a disposable cup, a length of yarn, and four different-colored counting bears. Have her make a circle with the yarn and place the cup beside it. Instruct students where to put the bears by giving them directions with positional words, such as "Put the yellow bear *inside* the cup." **Positional words**

✓ Label each of several paper bags with a different color word. Put in each bag magnetic letters that spell the corresponding word. Write a color word on a magnetic whiteboard. Have a student remove a letter from the corresponding bag and place it below the matching letter. Continue as described until each word is displayed. **Matching letters**

Copy the cards on page 16 so there is one card per student. Underline each word with the corresponding color and give a card to each student. Announce a color. Have any student holding a matching card stand and do the corresponding action. Continue as described with the other colors. **Word recognition**

Song

(sung to the tune of "Ten Little Indians")

Red crayons, blue crayons, yellow and purple crayons.
Brown crayons, black crayons, green and orange crayons.
Everyone whose favorite crayon is [red],
Please stand up and clap your hands!

Repeat the song several times, substituting different color words for *red*.

Phonemic awareness: Name the color words in the song that begin with *b*.

Journal Prompts

- Draw something yellow. Write and complete the following sentence: "I see a yellow _____."

- Draw something red. Write and complete the following sentence: "The _____ is red."

- Draw a dog. Write the following sentence and complete it with one or more color words: "The dog is _____."

- Draw something purple. Write about it.

- Draw something that is your favorite color. Write about it.

Instructions

Colorful Chats

Getting ready: Copy page 15 to make a class supply.

Steps:

1. Color the crayon your favorite color.
2. Draw a picture. Be sure to incorporate the crayon into your picture just as the illustrator does in the book.
3. Imagine what your crayon might say about your picture. Dictate a sentence for an adult to write.

Purple says, "Those grapes look yummy!"

Swirls of Color

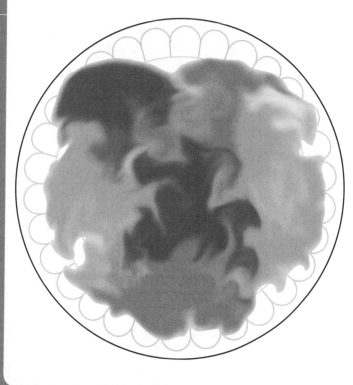

Materials for one project: paper plate, plastic food wrap, various colors of paint

Steps:

1. Squirt a few dots of primary-colored paint (two different colors) on the plate.
2. Place the plastic food wrap on the paint.
3. Put your fingers on the plastic food wrap and swirl the colors together.
4. Remove and discard the plastic food wrap. Allow the paint to dry.

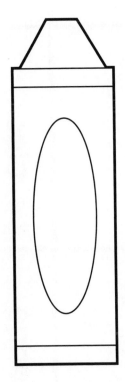

15

Color Word Cards

Use with the "Colors" unit on pages 11–14.

green

TEC61176

brown

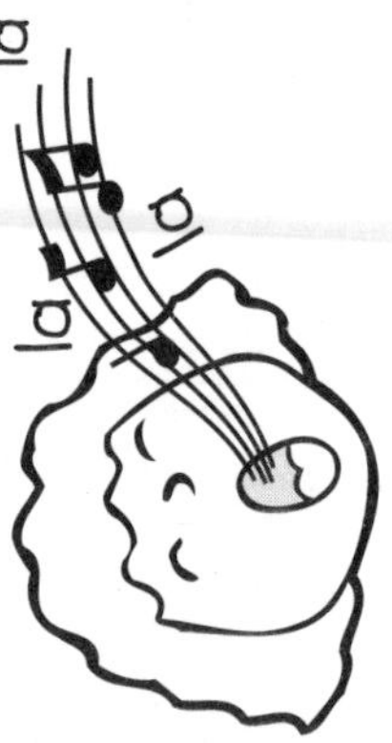

TEC61176

purple

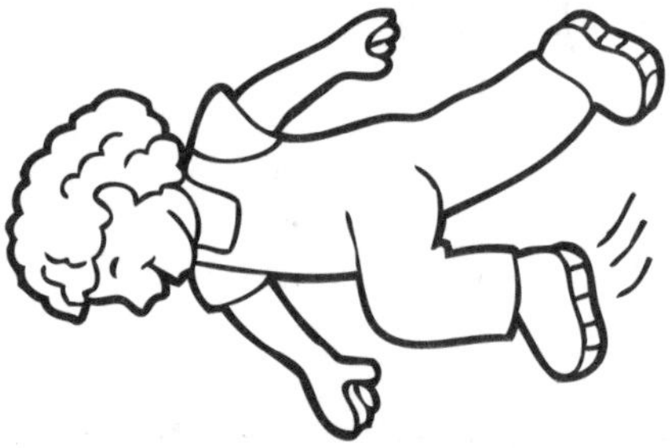

TEC61176

black

TEC61176

blue

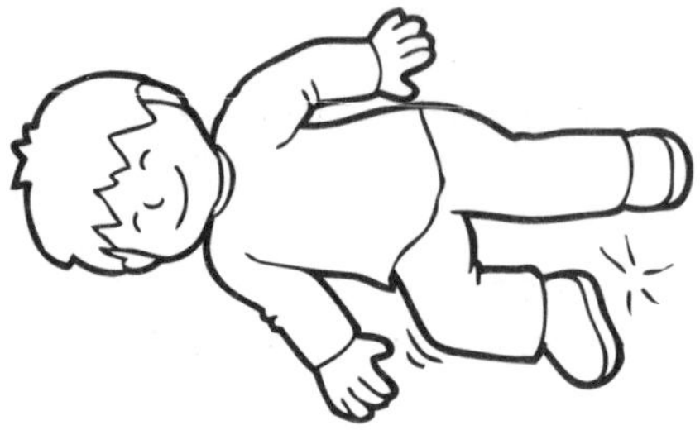

TEC61176

orange

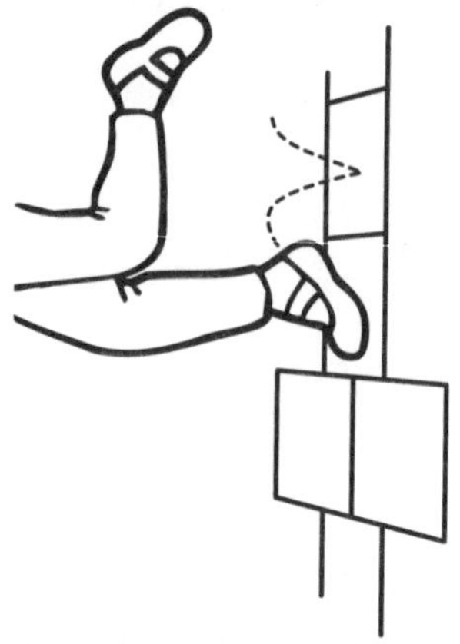

TEC61176

red

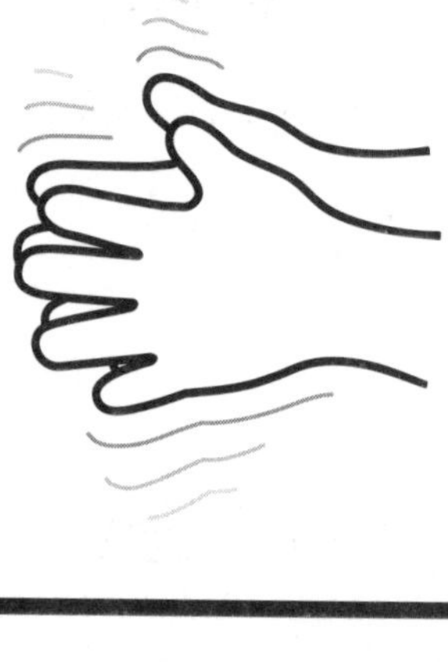

TEC61176

yellow

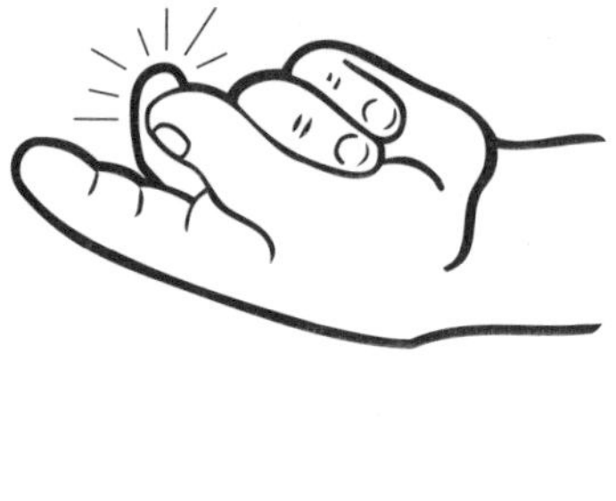

TEC61176

Day-by-Day Kindergarten Plans • ©The Mailbox® Books • TEC61176

Apples

Centers for the Week

ABC Center: Stock a container with letter manipulatives, including several uppercase and lowercase *a*'s. Set out an apple cutout labeled "A a" and a paper labeled with a sad face. A student puts the *a*'s on the apple and the other letters on the paper. *Letter recognition*

Reading Center: Write a high-frequency word on each of three brown rectangles (baskets). Write each word on a few apple cutouts, writing one word per apple. A student reads the apples and puts them on the matching baskets. *High-frequency words*

Math Center: Use different-colored pom-poms (apples) to make a pattern in the top row of a horizontal ice cube tray, leaving the last section or two empty. A student uses Unifix cubes to copy and extend the pattern in the empty row. *Patterning*

Fine-Motor Area: Set out colorful tagboard apples with holes punched along the edges and lengths of yarn in corresponding colors. Have students lace the cutouts. *Lacing*

Game Center: For this partner game, two players put 12 red counters (apples) on a tree cutout. Each player rolls a number cube and "picks" the corresponding number of apples. The players determine who has more apples. Then that player returns all the apples for another round. *Comparing sets*

Morning Group Time	Read-Alouds and Art

Monday

Attach an apple cutout to a craft stick to make a pointer. Write a message to students about the day's activities and draw an apple below it. After you read the message with students, use the pointer to help them count the words. Then write the corresponding number on the apple below the message. **Concepts about print**

Invite youngsters to briefly tell about their favorite apple products and any apple-picking experiences they have had. Then read aloud *Apples, Apples, Apples* by Nancy Elizabeth Wallace. **Prior knowledge**

Tuesday

Put a tree cutout on the floor. Arrange a class supply of personalized apple cutouts facedown on the tree. "Pick" an apple and read the name with students. Then ask the corresponding youngster to stand. After the group greets him, invite him to pick an apple to continue. After the last child has been greeted, invite him to lead the class in greeting an adult in the classsroom. **Name recognition**

Revisit the page in yesterday's book that shows the parts of an apple. Then have each child make an "Outside, Inside Apple." (See directions on page 20.) **Parts of an apple**

Ask me about these parts of an apple:
leaf
stem
skin
seeds
flesh

Wednesday

✓Give each child an apple cutout labeled with a number from 1 to 10. Then call a number and ask each child with a corresponding apple to stand. Have the seated students greet the youngsters with the chant below. Continue with the remaining numbers as described. **Number recognition**

> Good morning! Give a cheer!
> We're so glad [Sasha and Alex] are here.

Discuss with students the meaning of the word *balance*. Then invite each youngster to balance a paper plate on his head. After students talk about whether the task was easy or hard, read aloud *Ten Apples Up on Top!* by Theo. LeSieg. **Vocabulary**

Thursday

Write on chart paper "Today is [name of the day]. **Apple** begins with *a*. Find each *a* below." Then randomly write various letters, including several uppercase and lowercase *a*'s. Have students circle and count the *a*'s. **Letter knowledge**

Show students illustrations in yesterday's book that show characters balancing apples. Ask students to compare the number of apples the characters have, using words such as *more, fewer,* and *same as.* **Comparing sets**

Friday

✓Give each child a red, yellow, or green apple cutout. Instruct students to group themselves by apple color and then compare the number of apples in each group. **Comparing sets**

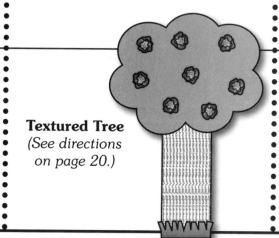

Textured Tree (See directions on page 20.)

Literacy and Math

✓ Have students taste pieces of red, green, and yellow apples. To show their apple preferences, help students make a graph in a pocket chart with red, green, and yellow rectangles. **Graphing**

Invite each child to dictate a sentence like the following: [Child's name] likes [color] apples." Write each sentence on chart paper. After students practice reading the sentences, include the writing in a student-illustrated class book. **Reading**

Ask several students to stand side by side with apple cutouts to form a color pattern. Once the seated students identify the pattern, ask volunteers to continue it. **Patterning**

✓ Display various apple cutouts in a pocket chart to form a different pattern in each row. Cover the last apple in each row with a blank card. Have students tell what comes next in each pattern. Remove the cards to reveal the correct answers. **Patterning**

✓ Color and cut out a copy of the picture cards on page 21. Put the tree and apple cards in a pocket chart to create column headings for one- and two-syllable words, respectively. Have students clap the syllables as they name the pictures on the remaining cards. Ask them to put the cards in the appropriate columns. **Phonological awareness**

Song

(sung to the tune of "She'll Be Comin' Round the Mountain")

Oh, we'll make some applesauce and apple pie. Yum! Yum!
Oh, we'll make some apple muffins, you and I. Yum! Yum!
Oh, we'll pick and peel some apples.
Then we'll cut and cook some apples.
Oh, we'll make some applesauce and apple pie. Yum! Yum!

Phonemic awareness: Guide students to notice that the words *pick* and *peel* have the same beginning sound, just as the words *cut* and *cook* do.

Journal Prompts

- Draw red and green apples. Write about them.

- Draw big and small apples. Write about them.

- Draw an apple. Write and complete the following sentence: "My apple is _____."

✓ Draw an apple tree and write about it.

- Draw things made with apples. Write about them.

Instructions

Outside, Inside Apple

Materials for one apple: apple-shaped booklet with red covers and one white page (no stem or leaves), booklet label like the one shown, green and brown paper scraps, scissors, glue, brown crayon

Steps:

1. Cut two leaves and a stem from scrap paper. Glue them to the booklet.
2. Draw apple seeds on the booklet page.
3. Glue the label to the front of the booklet.

Ask me about these parts of an apple:
leaf
stem
skin
seeds
flesh

Textured Tree

Materials for one tree: 3½" x 9" white paper, treetop cut from 9" x 12" green paper, 2-inch red tissue paper squares, 4-inch green crepe paper streamer, corrugated cardboard, brown crayon without a wrapper, glue, scissors

Steps:

1. To make a tree trunk, use the crayon to do a rubbing of the corrugated cardboard onto the white paper. Then glue the treetop to the trunk.
2. Crumple the tissue paper squares to make apples and then glue them to the treetop.
3. Snip one long side of the crepe paper streamer to make grass. Glue the grass to the bottom of the tree, keeping the snipped side free.

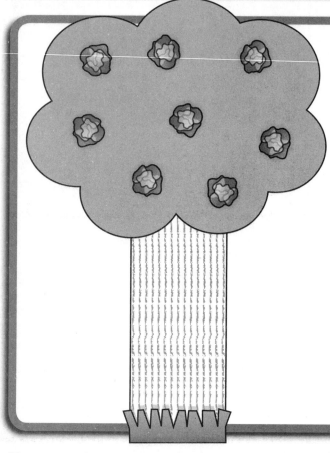

Name_____

Yum!

Write how many.

Circle the greater number.

Day-by-Day Kindergarten Plans • ©The Mailbox® Books • TEC61176

All About Me

Centers for the Week

ABC Center: Make a name card for each student. Set out a variety of supplies that can be used to spell names, such as letter tiles, magnetic letters, and play dough. A student uses his name card as a model and forms his name with different supplies. *Spelling names*

Reading Center: Gather a photo of each student and a corresponding name card. Code the backs of the matching photos and cards with identical stickers. Randomly display several photos and the matching name cards in a pocket chart. (Use the remaining photos and cards in later sessions.) A student matches the cards and photos. Then she flips them to check her work. *Reading names*

Math Center: Set out number cards, play dough, and birthday candles. A student chooses a number card. Then he makes a play dough birthday cake and puts the corresponding number of candles on the cake. He continues with the remaining cards as described. *Counting*

Art Center: Cut from magazines a class supply of pictures of eyes, noses, and mouths. Set out paper plates, crayons in different skin tones, yarn, and glue. To make a self-likeness, a student colors a plate and then glues selected details to it. *Self-awareness*

Science Center: On a large piece of paper, have each student make a handprint with washable ink and write her name near her print. Post the paper within students' reach and place a few magnifying glasses nearby. A student uses a magnifying glass to observe the likenesses and differences among the prints. *Making observations*

Morning Group Time	Read-Alouds and Art
Monday Have each student bring to school a photo of herself when she was younger. Share a photo with the class without identifying the student. Give students clues about the youngster and have them guess who it is. After you confirm the correct answer, continue with the remaining photos as described. *Listening skills*	Share with students the cover of *Chrysanthemum* by Kevin Henkes. Ask students to tell what they think a chrysanthemum is, encouraging them to use the cover illustration to guide their guesses. After you record students' guesses, read the book aloud. Then discuss students' guesses and the correct answer. *Prior knowledge*
Tuesday Tape to each student's shirt a construction paper badge labeled "I'm Special!" Then have students sit in a circle and pass a make-believe microphone around the circle. When a student receives the microphone, ask him to stand and say a complete sentence that tells one reason he is special. *Oral language*	Remind students that Chrysanthemum has a long name. Then give each student an adhesive nametag with the backing intact and assign her a partner. Have the students in each twosome compare the number of letters in their names. Then invite each student to decorate her nametag and wear it the rest of the day. *Number sense*
Wednesday Ask students to stand. Then give a clue about a secretly chosen student, such as "This student has brown hair." Have each student who does not fit the description sit down. Continue to give clues until only one child (the mystery student) is standing. *Listening skills*	**Nifty Names** *(See directions on page 26.)* 
Thursday Display an alphabet chart. Point to a letter and ask students to name it. Then have students whose names begin with that letter stand up. After you write the number of students beside the letter, ask the youngsters to sit down. Continue in this manner for each letter. Then discuss the results. *Letter knowledge, number sense* *How many students' names begin with B?*	Read aloud *ABC I Like Me!* by Nancy Carlson. Then give each student a copy of page 28. Have him write his name and then color the box containing the first letter of his name. Help him write and illustrate a sentence about himself. Bind the completed pages together to make a class book. *Written expression*
Friday To explore students' likes and dislikes, designate an area of the room for each of two different seasons, activities, or foods. Have each student choose the one he likes better and walk to the appropriate area. Then guide youngsters to determine which resulting group has more students and which group has fewer students. *Comparing sets*	**Me Collage** *(See directions on page 26.)* 

Literacy and Math

Tell students that some body parts come in pairs. Then draw a T chart on the board. Title one column "Pair" and the other column "Not a Pair." Guide students to name chosen body parts by giving clues, such as "We use these to see." Write the corresponding words in the appropriate columns with students' input. **Number sense**

✓ Instruct each student to look at his nametag and count the letters in his first name. Then help students form adjacent lines so each student with only two letters in his name is in one line, each student with three letters in his name is in the next line, and so on. After all students are in place, have them count and compare the number of children in each line. **Comparing sets**

Give each student a sheet of paper. Instruct him to draw himself doing an action, such as writing, clapping, or running. Then have him dictate a complete sentence naming the action and the part of his body used. Write the sentence below the picture. **Written expression**

I can draw with my hands.

Write each student's name on a slip of paper. Put the slips in a container. Then take two slips at random and have the corresponding students stand. Guide students to name one way the two youngsters are alike and one way they are different. Continue in this manner for the remaining names. **Comparing and contrasting**

Place a set of letters in a paper bag. Give each student a personalized sentence strip and several game markers. Take a letter at random, display it, and announce its name. Have each student with the letter in her name mark it on her sentence strip. Continue in this manner until a student marks all the letters in her name, stands, and says, "Name-O!" **Letter knowledge**

Song

✓

(sung to the tune of "Are You Sleeping?")

I am growing.
I am growing
Big and strong,
Big and strong.
Once I was a baby;
Now I am much bigger.
Yes, I am.
Yes, I am.

Word recognition: Display the song and have students count the number of times the word *I* appears in the song.

Journal Prompts

✓ • Draw your family and then label the picture.

✓ • Write and complete the following sentence: "I like to _____." Illustrate your sentence.

• Draw your favorite food. Write about it.

• Draw your favorite place. Write about it.

• Draw what you like to do after school. Write about it.

Nifty Names

Materials for one project: black construction paper with child's name written in chalk, shiny confetti, glue

Steps:
1. Squeeze a line of glue along each letter.
2. Sprinkle confetti on the glue, covering it completely.
3. Shake off the excess confetti.

Me Collage

Materials for one collage: copy of the person pattern on page 27, 12" x 18" sheet of construction paper, old magazines, construction paper scraps, yarn, markers, crayons, glue, scissors

Steps:
1. Vertically position your construction paper and write your name at the top of it.
2. Cut out the person pattern. Draw a face on the person and glue the cutout in the middle of your paper. Decorate the person to look like you using crayons, markers, paper scraps, and yarn.
3. Cut out magazine pictures of things you like. Glue the pictures to your paper.

Use with the "All About Me" unit on pages 23–26 and the read-aloud activity on page 12.

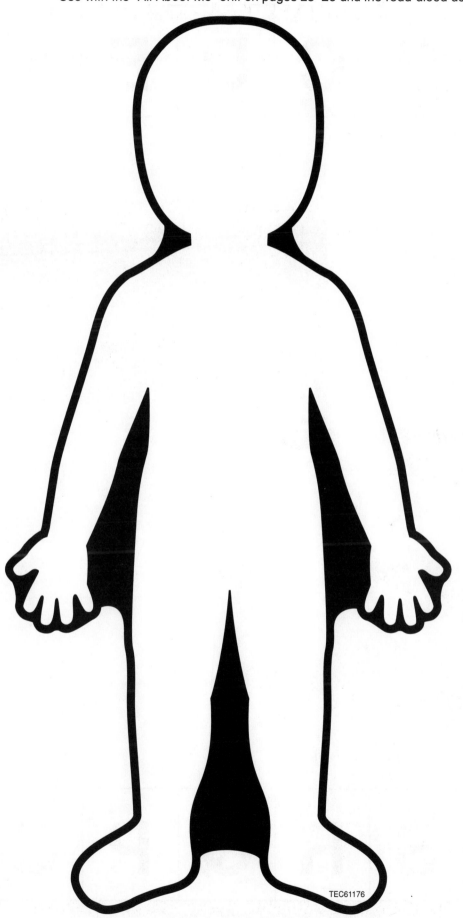

TEC61176

Name _____

A	B	C	D	E	F	G
Z						H
Y						I
X						J
W						K
V						L
U						M
T	S	R	Q	P	O	N

Note to the teacher: Use with the "All About Me" unit on pages 23–26.

Leaves

Centers for the Week

ABC Center: Set out a class supply of leaf cutouts (pattern on page 33), an ink pad, and letter stampers. A child finds the letter *l* stamper and stamps *l*'s on a leaf. ***Letter recognition***

Writing Center: Post a list of color words with the words written in the corresponding colors. A student draws and colors a leaf on a sheet of paper. She copies on the paper "My leaf is _____." Then she writes the appropriate color word in the blank. ***Color recognition***

Math Center: Set out a supply of leaf cutouts in three different shapes. A child sorts the leaves into piles according to shape. ***Sorting***

Art Center: Set out white paper, red fingerpaint, and yellow fingerpaint. A youngster fingerpaints on the paper with both colors of paint, observing the areas where the colors mix. After the paint dries, a child uses a tagboard leaf tracer (pattern on page 33) to cut a leaf from her paper. ***Color mixing***

Fine-Motor Center: Attach several leaves to a table using rolled pieces of tape. A child places a sheet of paper over the leaves and lightly tapes it in place. He rubs the side of a crayon over the paper, using different strokes (side to side and top to bottom) until all of the leaves have been revealed. ***Coloring***

Morning Group Time	Read-Alouds and Art
Monday Write a few sentences about leaves on a sheet of chart paper. Draw a green leaf at the beginning of each sentence and a red leaf at the end of each sentence. After you read the sentences aloud, invite volunteers to identify the beginning and end of each sentence. **Concepts of print** 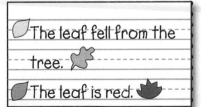	Invite youngsters to briefly share their favorite things about fall. Then read aloud *Fall Leaves Fall!* by Zoe Hall. **Prior knowledge**
Tuesday Give each student a red, a yellow, an orange, or a brown leaf cutout (pattern on page 33). On your signal, instruct youngsters to find classmates who have the same color leaf as they do. Have each group of students make a separate leaf pile in a designated area. **Sorting by color**	Revisit yesterday's story. Have each child glue a fall leaf onto a sheet of paper and incorporate it in a drawing. Help each child add a caption to her picture. **Written expression**
Wednesday Attach several leaf cutouts to a tree drawn on the board. Have volunteers use complete sentences to share something about fall as they remove a leaf from the tree. **Oral language**	Read aloud *Leaf Man* by Lois Ehlert. Then have each child collect a few leaves. Direct each child to glue the leaves to a sheet of paper to make a leaf person. Have each child count the number of leaves he used and help him write on his paper "I used [number] leaves to make my leaf person." **Counting**
Thursday On a sheet of chart paper, write "Today is [name of day]. We will talk about lovely fall leaves." Invite volunteers to circle each letter *l* in the message. **Letter recognition**	Revisit yesterday's story. Have each youngster draw a picture illustrating where he thinks the leaf man will land. Invite each child, in turn, to tell the class about his picture. **Oral language**
Friday Give each student a red, brown, or yellow leaf cutout. Help students use their cutouts to make a graph in a pocket chart. **Graphing**	**A Lovely Leaf** *(See directions on page 32.)* 

Literacy and Math

Draw a tree on the board. Number ten leaf cutouts and randomly attach them to the tree. Invite student volunteers to count backward from 10 to 1 by removing the leaves from the tree in descending order. ***Counting backward***

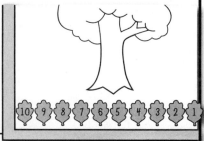

Have each child complete the activity "Lots of Leaves." (See directions on page 32.) ***Sorting***

Brainstorm with students words that begin with the same sound as *leaf*. Then play soft music as students pass a leaf cutout (pattern on page 33) around a circle. After a few moments, stop the music. Invite the child holding the leaf to name a word that begins with /l/. Then restart the music and play again. ***Beginning sound /l/***

In each row of a pocket chart, place three identical leaf cutouts and a leaf cutout that is different from the others. Ask students to identify the leaf that is different in each row and explain why it does not belong with the others. ***Visual discrimination***

On sentence strips, write simple sentences about leaves, featuring different color words. Display the strips in a pocket chart. Make leaf cutouts that correspond with each color word used in a sentence. Help students read each sentence and place the appropriate leaf beside the appropriate sentence strip. ***Reading color words***

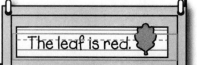

Song

(sung to the tune of "Old MacDonald Had a Farm")

Leaves are whirling, twirling down,
Falling from the tree!
Leaves are whirling, twirling down,
Falling down on me!
There's a [red] leaf here and a [red] leaf there.
Here a leaf, there a leaf,
Everywhere you see leaves.
Leaves are whirling, twirling down,
Falling from the tree!

Guide youngsters in singing the song several times, substituting different color words for the word *red*.

Phonological awareness: Write the song on chart paper. Have students circle the words *leaves* and *leaf*.

Journal Prompts

- Draw a leaf. Write and complete the following sentence: "My leaf is ___."

- Draw a pile of leaves. Write about it.

- Draw a tree with one leaf left on it. Write about the leaf.

- Draw a magical rake. Write about the things it can do.

- Draw a leaf falling from a tree. Write about how it feels.

Instructions

A Lovely Leaf

Materials for one leaf: brown paper leaf cutout (pattern on page 33), red and yellow tempera paint in squeeze bottles, craft stick

Steps:
1. Fold the leaf in half.
2. Open the leaf and squirt a few dabs of red and yellow paint on half of it.
3. Fold the leaf closed and gently rub the top to swirl the colors together.
4. To make veins, use a craft stick to "draw" a line along the fold and lines from the fold to the edge of the leaf.
5. Open the leaf and allow the paint to dry.

Lots of Leaves

Getting ready: Copy page 34 to make a class supply.

Steps:
1. Fold a 12" x 18" sheet of paper to create three sections.
2. Label one section "Small," one section "Medium," and one section "Large."
3. Color and cut out the cards.
4. Sort the leaves by size.
5. Glue the cards in the corresponding sections.

Small	Medium	Large

TEC61176

Leaf Cards

Use with the "Leaves" unit on pages 29–32.

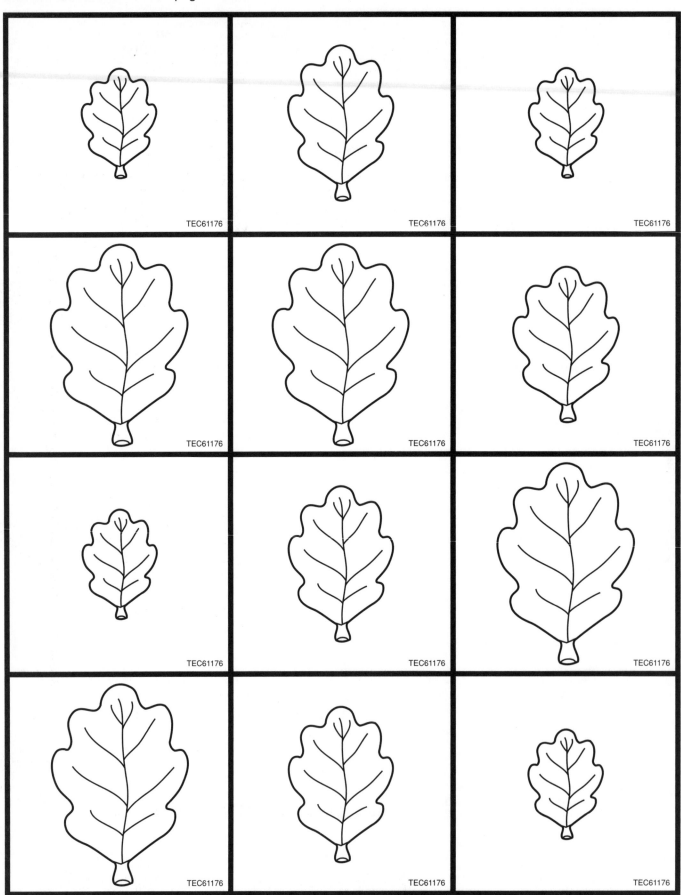

Day-by-Day Kindergarten Plans • ©The Mailbox® Books • TEC61176

Fire Safety

Centers for the Week

ABC Center: Label ten blue waterdrop cutouts with lowercase letters and ten red flame cutouts with the corresponding uppercase letters. A student matches a waterdrop to each flame. ***Matching uppercase and lowercase letters***

Reading Center: Program the dog's spots on a copy of page 39 with high-frequency words. Copy the page to make a class supply and place it at a center. A child reads the word on each spot and then traces around the spot with a black crayon. ***High-frequency words***

Math Center: For this partner center, cut strips from construction paper and label each resulting water hose with a number. Place the hoses at a center along with a waterdrop cutout. A child uses the waterdrop to point to and identify the number on each hose. After her partner verifies her answers, the two students switch roles. ***Number identification***

Fine-Motor Center: Use a marker to program pieces of plastic canvas with the numbers 911. Have youngsters use lengths of yarn to lace over the marker lines. ***Lacing***

Game Center: For this partner game, program 16 blank cards: four with a flame shape, four with "stop," four with "drop," and four with "roll." Stack the shuffled cards facedown. Partners take turns drawing cards, trying to collect one of each card. They return any duplicate cards to the bottom of the stack. Once a player has all four cards, he demonstrates how to stop, drop, and roll. ***Fire safety***

Morning Group Time	Read-Alouds and Art
Monday — Write a morning message on a sheet of chart paper. Read the message aloud, driving a toy fire truck (or a fire truck cutout) under each word as you read it. Then ask student volunteers to drive the truck to specific words in the message. **Concepts of print**	Invite students to share what they know about fire safety. Then read aloud *Safety Around Fire* by Lucia Raatma. **Prior knowledge**
Tuesday — Give a child a black cloud cutout (smoke) and hold a bell up high (smoke detector). Have the child hold the smoke near the floor and slowly raise it up to demonstrate that smoke rises. Ring the bell when the smoke gets near it. Then guide youngsters to demonstrate how to stay low and crawl to escape the smoke from a fire. **Science**	Revisit yesterday's book. Discuss with students the difference between good fires and bad fires. Have youngsters share what they learned about staying safe around both kinds of fires. **Restating important information**
Wednesday — On the board, draw a ladder leading to a window with flames. Write a number on each rung of the ladder. Invite youngsters to identify each number. When students reach the window, have them put out the fire by squirting imaginary hoses as you erase the flames. **Number identification** 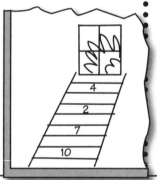	Read aloud *Firefighters! Speeding! Spraying! Saving!* by Patricia Hubbell. This book follows a group of firefighters as they are called to fight a fire. After sharing the story, pretend that a fire alarm is ringing and conduct a fire drill. **Fire safety**
Thursday — Name different household items, including several that pose a risk of fire or burns, such as matches, candles, and a stove. As you announce each item, if it is safe to touch, have youngsters hold up both hands and announce, "Safe to touch—very much!" If an item is not safe to touch, have children keep their hands in their laps and say, "Might be hot—better not!" **Science**	Revisit yesterday's story. As you review each page with students, invite volunteers to share the rhyming words they hear on each page. **Rhyming**
Friday — Play a game of The Firefighter Says. Wear a plastic firefighter helmet (or hold a firefighter cutout) and give students one- or two-step directions to follow. Once students are familiar with the game, invite volunteers to take turns being the firefighter. **Following directions**	**Firefighters' Friend** *(See directions on page 38.)* 

Literacy and Math

For this small-group activity, make a copy of page 39 for each child. To make gameboards, randomly label the spots on each dog with different numbers and then give a gameboard to each child. To play Doggy Lotto, announce one of the numbers from the gameboards and have youngsters color each spot with that number black. Continue until each child has colored all the spots on his dog. ***Number recognition***

Label house cutouts with letters and place them in a pocket chart. Hide a flame cutout behind a house. A child names a letter and looks for the flame behind the corresponding house. If she finds the flame, she pretends to put out the fire and then hides the flame for the next round of play. If she does not, another volunteer takes a turn. ***Letter identification***

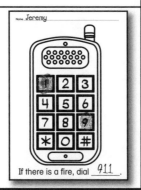

Invite students to help generate a list of words that can describe a fire truck. Post the completed list. Then have each child draw a fire truck and use the words on the list to write a sentence about it. ***Writing***

Place an alphabet strip on the floor. Say a letter aloud and invite a child to "drive" a toy fire truck to that letter on the strip. ***Letter recognition***

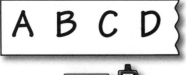

Have each child complete the activity **"Know the Number!"** (See directions on page 38.) ***Writing numbers***

Song

(sung to the tune of "Row, Row, Row Your Boat")

Make a safety plan. Practice till you
   know
If there is a lot of smoke, stop, stay low,
   and go.
Make a safety plan. Practice everyone!
Meet outside where you'll be safe; then
   call 9-1-1!

Fire safety: After leading youngsters in singing the song, discuss the important safety information featured in the song. Talk about fire safety prevention techniques, such as how to make a safety plan, what children should do if they see smoke or a fire, and what phone number to dial to report a fire.

Journal Prompts

- Draw a firefighter. Write about some things that firefighters do.

- Draw what you should do if your clothing catches fire. Write a sentence to describe your drawing.

- Draw a fire. Write about what you should do if you see a fire.

- Draw a smoke detector. Write about how it can help keep you safe.

- Write about something you have learned about fire safety. Illustrate your writing.

Firefighters' Friend

Materials for one dalmatian: 6" x 9" sheets of white and red construction paper, scissors, crayons, glue

Steps:
1. Remove your shoe (keep your sock on) and place your foot on the white paper. Ask a friend to trace around your foot.
2. Cut out your foot tracing.
3. Cut ears and a tail from the white paper scraps.
4. Glue the cutouts to the red paper as shown.
5. Draw spots and other details to complete the dog.

Know the Number!

Getting ready: Copy page 40 to make a class supply. Set out several ink pads.

Steps:
1. Trace each number and symbol on the telephone.
2. Practice pressing 9-1-1 on the phone.
3. After you have practiced a few times, press the numbers again, this time making ink fingerprints on the appropriate numbers.
4. Complete the sentence at the bottom of the page.

Name _____

Day-by-Day Kindergarten Plans • ©The Mailbox® Books • TEC61176

Note to the teacher: Use with the "Fire Safety" unit on pages 35–38.

Name _____

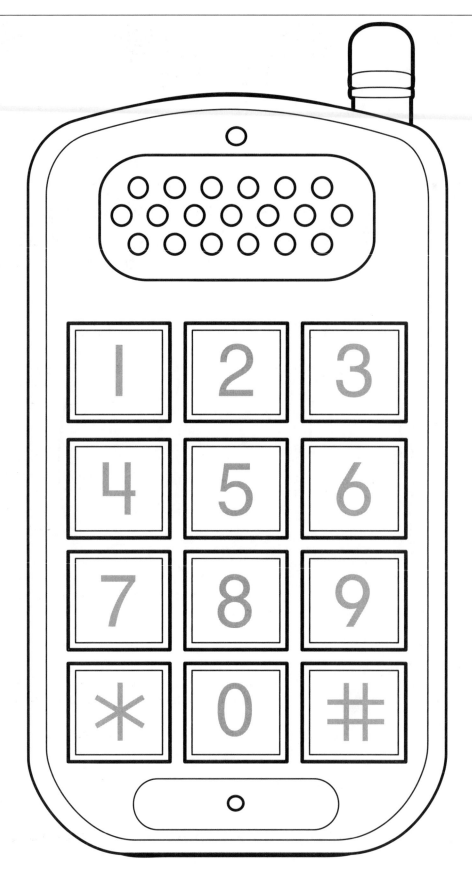

If there is a fire, dial _____.

Day-by-Day Kindergarten Plans • ©The Mailbox® Books • TEC61176

40   **Note to the teacher:** Use with the "Fire Safety" unit on pages 35–38.

Pumpkins

Centers for the Week

ABC Center: Gather letter manipulatives, including several uppercase and lowercase *p*'s. Place them at a center along with a plastic pumpkin bucket. A student places the *p*'s in the pumpkin bucket and sets the other letters aside. *Letter recognition*

Reading Center: Label a seed cutout "1" and a pumpkin cutout "2." Place the cutouts at a center along with picture cards that illustrate one- and two-syllable words. A child chooses a card and claps the number of word parts in the word. If it has one syllable like *seed,* he places the card on the seed. If it has two word parts like *pumpkin,* he places the card on the pumpkin. *Phonological awareness*

Math Center: Number 20 pumpkin seed cutouts from 1 to 20 and place them in an empty pumpkin seed packet. A child empties the packet and then places the seeds in order. *Number order*

Fine-Motor Center: Place a variety of shape tracers at a center. A youngster uses a white crayon to trace the shapes of his choosing onto black construction paper. Then he cuts out the shapes and glues them to a large pumpkin cutout to create a jack-o'-lantern. *Tracing, cutting, and gluing*

Science Center: Set out a small pumpkin and another small pumpkin that you have cut in half. Provide magnifying glasses, paper, and crayons. A student examines the inside and outside of the pumpkins and then draws what he sees. *Recording observations*

Morning Group Time	Read-Alouds and Art
Monday On chart paper write, "*Pumpkin* starts with *p*. Find the *p*'s below." Write an assortment of letters, including several uppercase and lowercase *p*'s, below the message. Invite student volunteers to circle each *p* with an orange marker and then add a green marker stem so that it resembles a pumpkin. ***Letter recognition***	Read aloud *The Biggest Pumpkin Ever* by Steven Kroll. Have each student write about what he would do to grow the biggest pumpkin ever and then add an illustration. ***Writing***

Monday

On chart paper write, "*Pumpkin* starts with *p*. Find the *p*'s below." Write an assortment of letters, including several uppercase and lowercase *p*'s, below the message. Invite student volunteers to circle each *p* with an orange marker and then add a green marker stem so that it resembles a pumpkin. ***Letter recognition***

Read aloud *The Biggest Pumpkin Ever* by Steven Kroll. Have each student write about what he would do to grow the biggest pumpkin ever and then add an illustration. ***Writing***

Tuesday

Draw a long vine on the board. Number 20 pumpkin cutouts (pattern on page 45) from 1 to 20. Tape some of the pumpkins on the board, leaving spaces for the missing pumpkins. Ask students to determine the missing numbers and then attach the appropriate pumpkins in the corresponding locations. ***Number order***

Three-Dimensional Pumpkin
(See directions on page 44.) Revisit yesterday's story. Then have each student make a pumpkin.

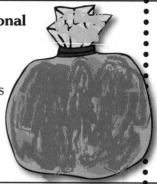

Wednesday

Attach a pumpkin cutout (pattern on page 45) to a craft stick to make a pointer. Invite volunteers to use the pointer to indicate items in the room that begin with the /p/ sound as in *pumpkin*. ***Beginning sound /p/***

Read aloud *Five Little Pumpkins* by Iris Van Rynbach. Give each of five students a pumpkin cutout (pattern on page 45) labeled with an ordinal number from *1st* to *5th*. As you revisit the story, invite the students with pumpkins to arrange themselves in order in front of the group. ***Ordinal numbers***

Thursday

Give each student a pumpkin cutout (pattern on page 45). Have each child follow your directions as you ask her to put her pumpkin *above* and *on* her head, *under* her foot, *next to* her leg, or *over* her hand. ***Positional words***

Encourage youngsters to share what they know about how a pumpkin grows as you record their responses on the board. Read aloud *It's Pumpkin Time!* by Zoe Hall. Then lead a discussion comparing students' ideas to the information presented in the book. ***Prior knowledge***

Friday

Set out a large pumpkin. Cut a length of string for each child that is either shorter than, longer than, or the same size as the circumference of the pumpkin. Give each child a length of string and have him predict whether his string will be too short, just right, or too long when placed around the middle of the pumpkin. Then have students take turns measuring the pumpkin with their strings. ***Measurement***

Jolly Jack-o'-Lantern
(See directions on page 44.)

Literacy and Math

Ask each youngster to make three different-size pumpkins from orange play dough. Then have him line up his pumpkins from smallest to largest. For an added challenge, pair students and have each duo order its six pumpkins. ***Ordering by size***

Give each child a copy of page 46. Have her write two words that describe pumpkins. Then invite her to illustrate her sentence and cut out the circle. Bind the completed pages between two pumpkin-shaped construction paper covers with the title "Describing Pumpkins." ***Writing***

Place a large supply of orange pom-poms on a piece of green bulletin board paper to make a pumpkin patch. Invite a child to roll a die and "pick" the corresponding number of pumpkins from the patch. Continue until the pumpkin patch is empty. ***Counting***

Ask each child to draw a vine and leaves on a paper strip. Announce a pair of words. If the words rhyme, have each child use an orange bingo dauber or crayon to add a pumpkin to his vine. If they do not rhyme, he does nothing. Continue as time allows. ***Rhyming***

Draw a jack-o'-lantern on the board using different shapes for the eyes, nose, and mouth. Have volunteers name the shapes. Then repeat the activity by making new faces with different shapes. ***Shape identification***

Song

(sung to the tune of "Take Me Out to the Ballgame")

Take me out in October!
Take me out to a farm!
Find me a pumpkin fat as can be;
I'd like one even bigger than me!
Yes, it's pumpkin time in October,
My favorite time of the year!
Oh! It just could never be fall
Without pumpkins here!

Phonemic awareness: Guide youngsters in naming each word in the song that begins with *f*.

Journal Prompts

- Draw a pumpkin seed. Write about what happens to a pumpkin seed after it is planted.

- Draw things made using pumpkin. Write about them.

- Draw the inside of a pumpkin. Write about it.

- Draw a jack-o'-lantern. Write to describe it.

- Complete the following sentence: "The pumpkin grew so big that…" Then illustrate your sentence.

Instructions

Three-Dimensional Pumpkin

Materials for one pumpkin: newspaper strips, lunch-size paper bag, rubber band, orange and green tempera paint, paintbrush

Steps:
1. Stuff the bag with newspaper strips.
2. Twist the open end of the bag to make a stem and secure it with a rubber band.
3. Paint the bag so that it resembles a pumpkin.

Jolly Jack-o'-Lantern

Materials for one jack-o'-lantern: sheet of black construction paper; orange, yellow, and green tissue paper scraps; chalk; diluted glue; paintbrush

Steps:
1. On a sheet of black paper, draw a chalk circle.
2. Brush diluted glue inside the circle.
3. Press pieces of torn orange tissue paper on the glue.
4. Glue torn green tissue paper to the top of the circle to make a stem.
5. When the glue is dry, tear yellow tissue paper scraps to make facial features and glue them to the pumpkin to make a jack-o'-lantern.

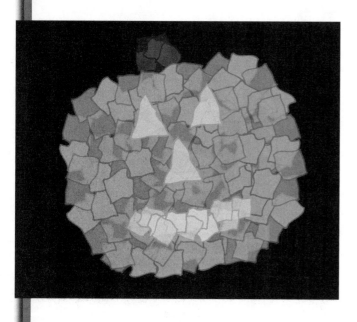

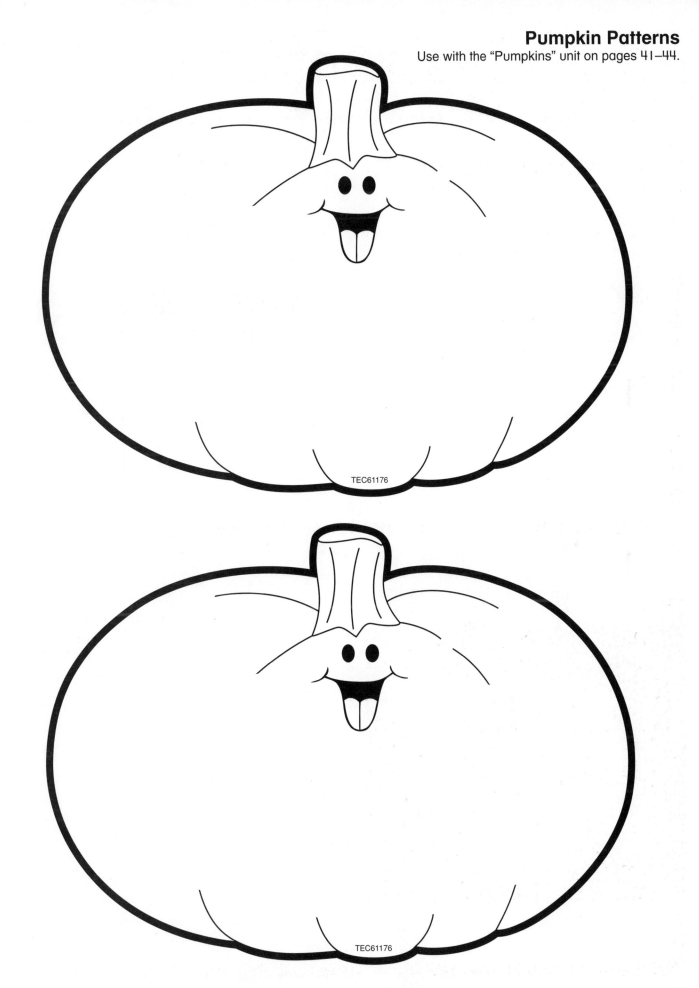

TEC61176

TEC61176

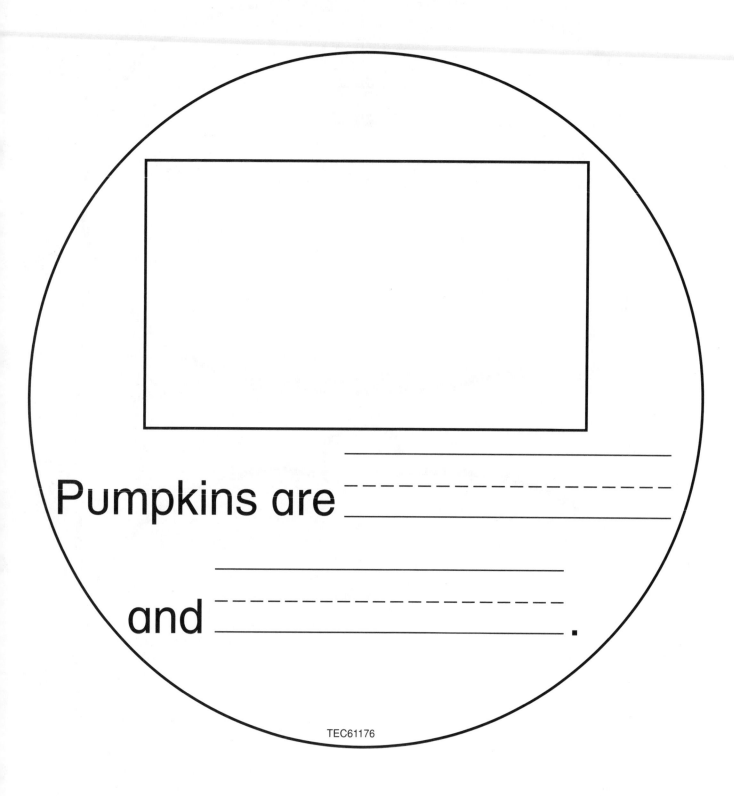

Pumpkins are _____

and _____ .

TEC61176

Spiders and Bats

Centers for the Week

ABC Center: On a sheet of poster board, draw a spiderweb. Using a different color, write several letters on the web. A child tosses a beanbag on the web, identifies the letter it lands on or closest to, and then makes the appropriate letter sound. ***Letter-sound association***

Reading Center: Label a bat cutout (pattern on page 51) and glue it on a large sheet of construction paper. Place nearby a set of word cards, including several with words that end in -*at*. (If desired, add pictures to the cards.) A youngster reads the word on each card. He places each -*at* word card on the bat and sets the remaining cards aside. ***Word family: -at***

Math Center: Draw a spiderweb on a paper plate. Place the web, a supply of pom-poms (bugs), and a set of number cards at a center. A child chooses a card and then places the corresponding number of bugs on the web. ***Making sets***

Art Center: Set out black ink pads and fine-tip markers. A youngster makes black fingerprint "spiders" on a sheet of paper and then uses a marker to add eight legs to each one. ***Counting***

Fine-Motor Center: Tie a length of yarn between two chairs. Number ten upside-down bat cutouts (pattern on page 51) from 1 to 10. A child uses clothespins to clip each bat to the yarn in order. ***Pincer grasp, number order***

Morning Group Time	Read-Alouds and Art
Monday — Give each child a plastic spider ring or a spider cutout (pattern on page 51). Use positional words to give her instructions on where to place her spider in relation to parts of her body. ***Positional words***	Read aloud *Stellaluna* by Janell Cannon. Revisit the pages in the story where Stellaluna attempts to land on a branch and becomes embarrassed. Discuss with students what it means to be embarrassed. Then have each child draw a picture of a time he was embarrassed and add a caption to his illustration. ***Writing a caption***
Tuesday — In turn, ask each child to identify a letter on a card. After he identifies the letter, invite him to "fly" to the "bat cave" (a designated area in the room). When each student is in the cave, invite all your little bats to fly out! ***Letter identification***	**High-Flying Bats** *(See directions on page 50.)* 
Wednesday — Invite each child to choose whether she prefers spiders or bats. Place a spider cutout and a bat cutout (patterns on page 51) in the top row of a pocket chart. Then help students use name cards to make a graph displaying their preferences. ***Graphing***	Read aloud *The Very Busy Spider* by Eric Carle. Sit with children in a circle and hold the end of a ball of yarn while rolling it to a student. The student tells what he would like to ask the spider to do with him. Then he holds the yarn with one hand and rolls the ball to a classmate. Continue until a yarn web has been made. ***Oral language***
Thursday — Read aloud the nursery rhyme "Little Miss Muffet." Have each pair of students think of something different for Miss Muffet to do when the spider sits beside her. Then invite each pair, in turn, to perform its new version of the nursery rhyme. ***Oral language***	Read aloud *Miss Spider's Tea Party* by David Kirk. Then revisit each page in the story and lead students in counting the number of characters or items illustrated on each page. ***Counting***
Friday — Line up ten cave cutouts; then hide a bat cutout (pattern on page 51) behind one. Have a youngster use an ordinal number to guess which cave the bat is hiding in. Continue in this manner until the bat's hiding place has been revealed. ***Ordinal numbers***	**A Spooky Spider** *(See directions on page 50.)* 

Literacy and Math

Set out a bat cutout and a spider cutout (patterns on page 51). Announce a one- or two-syllable word. Invite students to clap the word parts as they repeat the word. If the word has one syllable like *bat*, invite youngsters to flap their arms like a bat. If the word has two syllables like *spider*, have students move their fingers to imitate crawling like a spider. ***Phonological awareness***

Draw a large cave on the board. Post a desired number of bat cutouts (pattern on page 51) inside the cave. A volunteer counts the bats and writes the corresponding number on the board. Then she posts a different number of bats in the cave for another child to count. ***Counting, number formation***

For this partner activity, give each child a cave cutout and six black pom-poms (bats). In turn, each partner rolls a die and places the corresponding number of bats in his cave. The partners compare the number of bats in the caves and determine which has more or whether the two caves have an equal number of bats. Then they remove the bats to repeat the activity. ***Comparing sets***

Post a bat cutout and a spider cutout (patterns on page 51) above a Venn diagram. Invite volunteers to share facts about bats and spiders. Then guide students in determining in which section of the Venn diagram each fact should be written. ***Comparing and contrasting***

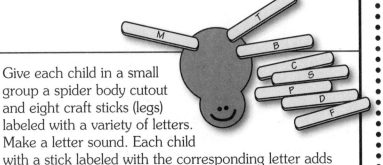

Give each child in a small group a spider body cutout and eight craft sticks (legs) labeled with a variety of letters. Make a letter sound. Each child with a stick labeled with the corresponding letter adds it to her spider. Play continues until a child has placed eight legs on her spider. ***Letter-sound association***

Song

(sung to the tune of "I Have a Little Dreidel")

There is a little spider; he's good in
   every way.
I like that little spider, for he eats bugs
   all day!

There is a little brown bat; he's such a
   welcome sight!
I like that little brown bat, for he eats
   bugs all night!

The brown bat and the spider both help
   my garden grow.
They both can catch and eat up bad
   garden bugs, you know!

Phonological awareness: After leading youngsters in singing the song, invite volunteers to name pairs of rhyming words they hear in the song.

Journal Prompts

- Draw a bat and then write something you know about bats.

- Draw a bat flying at night. Write to tell where it is going.

- Draw a spider and then write something you know about spiders.

- Draw a spiderweb without a spider. Write about where the spider is and what it is doing.

- Draw a bat and a spider. Write one thing that is different about the two critters.

High-Flying Bats

Materials for one project: 9" yellow construction paper circle, three 2" black construction paper circles, three 2" black construction paper squares, white crayon, scissors, glue

Steps:
1. Cut each square in half to make two triangles (wings).
2. Glue one black circle (head) between each pair of triangles to make three bats.
3. Use the crayon to add details to the bats.
4. Glue the bats to the yellow circle (moon).
5. If desired, create a mobile by hole-punching the moon and adding a length of yarn for hanging.

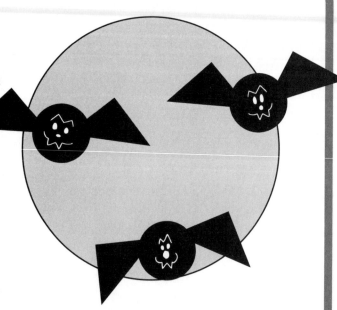

A Spooky Spider

Materials for one spider: 5" and 9" tagboard circle tracers, 12" x 18" sheet of black construction paper, eight 1" x 9" construction paper strips, 2 sticky dots, white crayon, scissors, glue

Steps:
1. Use the crayon to trace both circle tracers on the black paper. Cut out the tracings.
2. Glue the small circle (head) to the large circle (body).
3. Accordion-fold each paper strip.
4. Glue four strips to each side of the spider's body to make legs.
5. Add sticky dot eyes to the small circle. Then use the crayon to add details to make the spider's face.

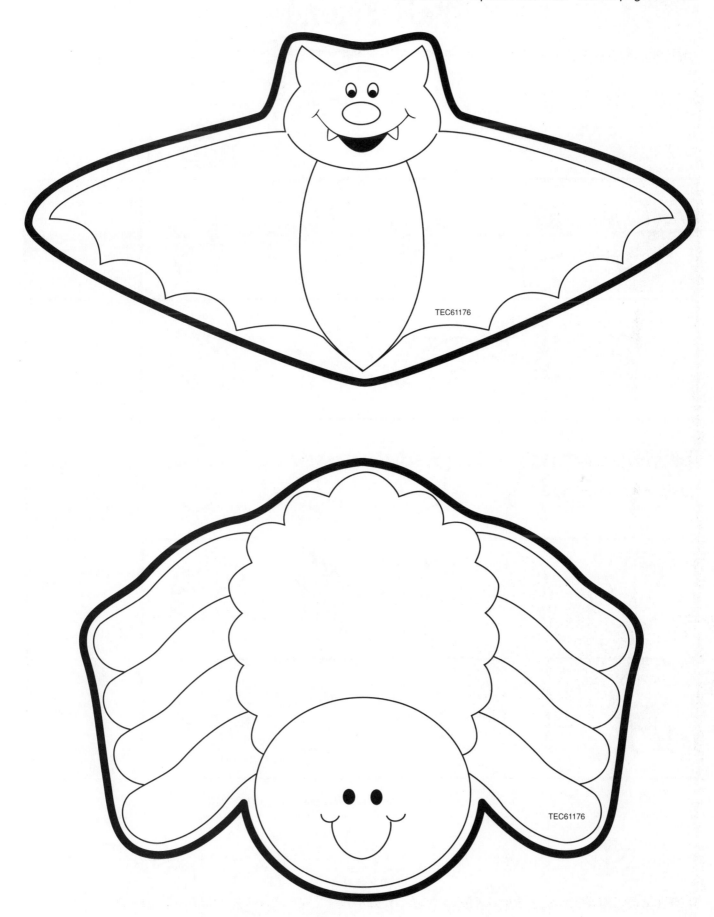

TEC61176

TEC61176

Name_____

Fall Friends

What comes next?

 Cut.

Glue.

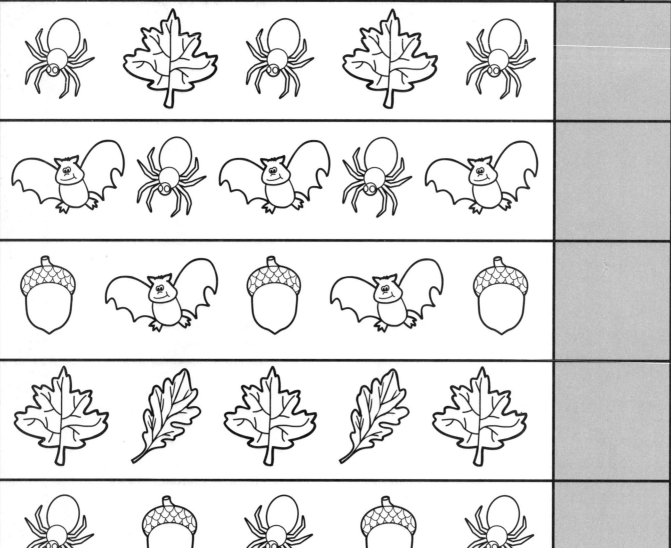

52

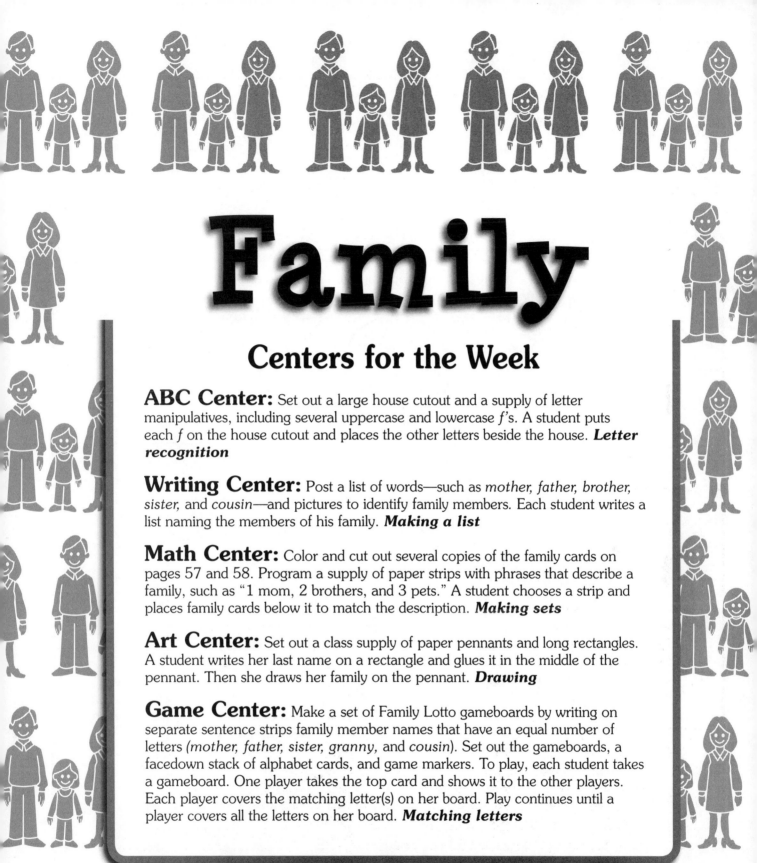

Family

Centers for the Week

ABC Center: Set out a large house cutout and a supply of letter manipulatives, including several uppercase and lowercase *f*'s. A student puts each *f* on the house cutout and places the other letters beside the house. ***Letter recognition***

Writing Center: Post a list of words—such as *mother, father, brother, sister,* and *cousin*—and pictures to identify family members. Each student writes a list naming the members of his family. ***Making a list***

Math Center: Color and cut out several copies of the family cards on pages 57 and 58. Program a supply of paper strips with phrases that describe a family, such as "1 mom, 2 brothers, and 3 pets." A student chooses a strip and places family cards below it to match the description. ***Making sets***

Art Center: Set out a class supply of paper pennants and long rectangles. A student writes her last name on a rectangle and glues it in the middle of the pennant. Then she draws her family on the pennant. ***Drawing***

Game Center: Make a set of Family Lotto gameboards by writing on separate sentence strips family member names that have an equal number of letters (*mother, father, sister, granny,* and *cousin*). Set out the gameboards, a facedown stack of alphabet cards, and game markers. To play, each student takes a gameboard. One player takes the top card and shows it to the other players. Each player covers the matching letter(s) on her board. Play continues until a player covers all the letters on her board. ***Matching letters***

Morning Group Time	Read-Alouds and Art
Monday Label a copy of the family cards on pages 57 and 58 with the nouns they represent, such as "grandpa," "aunt," and "sister." Cut out the cards and place them in a basket. Invite each child to choose a card and tell something about the relative represented. If a student does not have a relative like the one represented, he chooses another card. **Oral language**	Invite each youngster to tell about a relative that does not live with him. Then read aloud *Climb the Family Tree, Jesse Bear!* by Nancy White Carlstrom. **Prior knowledge**
Tuesday Have each student draw a smiley face on a construction paper circle. Ask questions such as, "Does your family like to ride bikes?" or "Does your family have pets?" To answer yes, a youngster raises her smiley face. **Listening**	Revisit yesterday's book. Complete "Family Tree Fun" (see directions on page 56) to review the different things Jesse Bear's family members do during their reunion. **Recalling events**
Wednesday Lead students in singing the song below several times, changing the underlined word to a different family member each time. **Family structure** *(sung to the tune of "Did You Ever See a Lassie?")* Oh, if you have a [sister], a [sister], a [sister], Oh, if you have a [sister], Will you raise your hand?	Read aloud *Rattletrap Car* by Phyllis Root. Stop reading each time the car breaks down and ask students to predict how this resourceful family will fix the car. **Making predictions**
Thursday Designate an area of the classroom for each of the following categories: only child, oldest child, middle child, and youngest child. Then instruct each student to walk to the area of the room that matches his birth order. Lead students in counting and comparing the groups. **Sorting**	Revisit yesterday's story and discuss how the family members work together to solve their problems. Invite each student to share a time when her family members worked together. **Making connections**
Friday Have students sit in a circle. Pass a toy camera to a student. Instruct her to stand and tell her classmates about an activity her family members enjoy doing together. Then have her sit down and pass the camera to the next student. Continue until each student has had a turn. **Oral language**	**A Family Home** *(See directions on page 56.)* 

Literacy and Math

For each child, write on a sentence strip "[Child]'s family has [number] people." Give each child her strip and have her glue it to a large sheet of paper. Direct her to illustrate the sentence. Collect the finished pages and bind them together to make a book. ***Illustrating a sentence***

Label the columns of a graph with the following: *2, 3, 4, 5,* and *6 or more.* Instruct each student to write her name on an index card. Then have her put the card in the column that corresponds with the number of people in her family. When the graph is complete, direct students to count and compare the columns. ***Graphing***

Ask students to share some of the chores they do at home. Then have each child make a few handprints with paint on a sheet of paper. When the paint is dry, help him write on each handprint a different way he helps his family. ***Writing***

Copy and cut out a supply of the family cards on pages 57 and 58. Invite a volunteer to use the family members to make a simple pattern. Ask another student to name the pattern. Continue until each student has had a turn to make or name a pattern. ***Patterning***

Ask students to think about rules they have at home. Have each child write about and illustrate one of his family's rules. Provide time for students to share their rules. Then lead students in determining which rules are most common. ***Writing***

Song

(sung to the tune of "Did You Ever See a Lassie?")

Everybody needs a family, a family, a family.
Everybody needs a family to help them each day.
A family protects us. A family respects us.
Everybody needs a family to help them each day.

Print concepts: Display a copy of the song. Invite volunteers to locate and circle all the periods.

Journal Prompts

- Write and complete the following sentence: I like my family because _____. Illustrate the sentence.

- Draw yourself helping a family member. Write about it.

- Draw a family member who is older than you. Write about this person.

- Draw your family doing a favorite activity. Write about it.

- Write and complete the following sentence: My family is special because _____. Illustrate your sentence.

Instructions

Family Tree Fun

Getting ready: Cut out a light green paper leaf for each student. Post a large tree minus foliage in a location that is easily accessible to students.

Steps:
1. On the leaf, draw an event that happens during Jesse Bear's family reunion. (See Monday's read-aloud on page 54.)
2. Tell about your drawing.
3. Attach your leaf to the tree.

A Family Home

Materials for one project: copy of a family photograph, personalized house cutout with a precut door flap, sheet of light blue construction paper, tape, glue, crayons

Steps:
1. Color and decorate the house as desired.
2. Tape the photo to the back of the house so it is seen when the door flap is open.
3. Glue the house on light blue construction paper.
4. Add desired details around the house.

TEC6176
TEC6176
TEC6176
TEC6176
TEC6176
TEC6176
TEC6176

Family Cards

Use with the "Family" unit on pages 53–56.

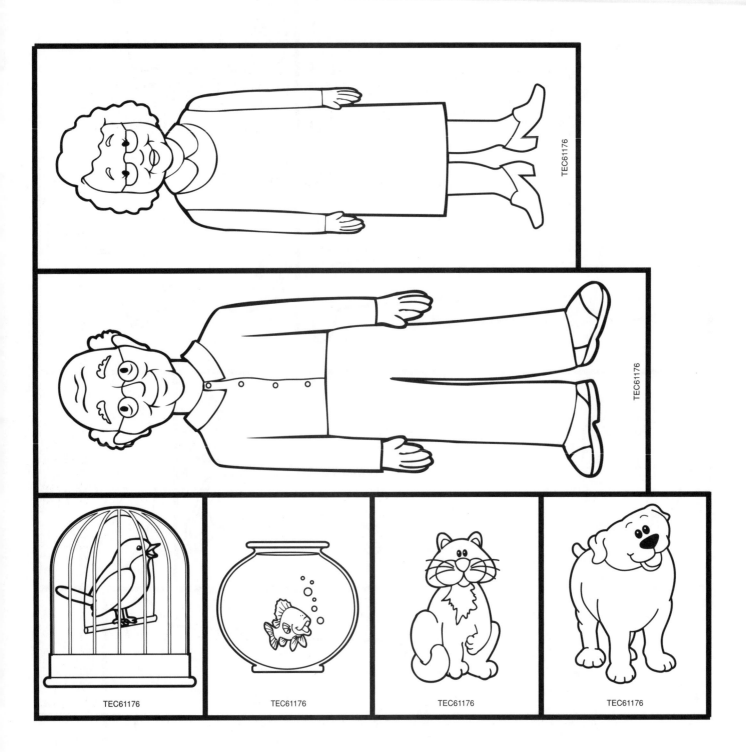

TEC61176

TEC61176

TEC61176

TEC61176

TEC61176

TEC61176

Scarecrows

Centers for the Week

Reading Center: Program cornstalk cutouts with high-frequency words. On a supply of corn cutouts (pattern on page 69), write the same words. A student reads the word on each ear of corn and then places it on the corresponding stalk. ***High-frequency words***

Writing Center: On a haystack cutout, list words with picture cues to make a word bank for describing a scarecrow. Consider words such as *hat, straw, patch, pants,* and *shirt.* Post the haystack at a center. A student draws a scarecrow on a sheet of paper and then uses the word bank to write about his drawing. ***Descriptive words***

Math Center: Label each of several large sheets of brown paper (fields) with a different number. Place the fields at a center along with a supply of black pom-poms (crows). A child reads the number on each field and then places that many crows on it. ***Counting***

Art Center: Set out shirt and pant tracers, wrapping paper scraps, and several colors of blank paper. A student traces pants and a shirt on blank paper, cuts them out, and glues them on another sheet of paper. Next, he cuts wrapping paper patches and glues them to the scarecrow's clothes. Then he draws the rest of his scarecrow. ***Tracing, cutting, drawing***

Game Center: For this partner game, set out an enlarged copy of the scarecrow pattern on page 63, a die, and 20 small paper patches. In turn, a student rolls the die and places the corresponding number of patches on the scarecrow. Partners continue until there are no more patches. Then they count the total number of patches on the scarecrow. ***Counting***

Morning Group Time	Read-Alouds and Art
Monday Share with students the reason why farmers put scarecrows in their fields. Then invite youngsters to brainstorm other ways that farmers could scare the crows out of their fields. Make a list of their suggestions on the board. *Oral language*	Read aloud *The Little Scarecrow Boy* by Margaret Wise Brown. Invite students to discuss a time they wanted to do something but were told they must wait until they are older. *Making connections*
Tuesday Have students stand in a circle to do a scarecrow version of "The Hokey-Pokey." When singing, replace the body parts used in "The Hokey-Pokey" with right glove, left glove, right boot, left boot, and floppy hat. *Right and left, following directions*	Ask students to name types of clothes scarecrows wear. Then show students the cover of *Waltz of the Scarecrows* by Constance W. McGeorge. Have students predict why the scarecrows on the cover are dressed in fancy clothing. Read the story aloud and have students check their predictions. *Prior knowledge, making predictions*
Wednesday Ask five or more students to pretend to be crows and line up side by side facing the class. Have each crow state her ordinal position in line. Then play the role of a scarecrow and say, "Boo!" At this signal, each child changes her place in line. Then have the seated students answer questions about the crows' ordinal positions. *Ordinal numbers*	Discuss with students the meaning of the word *trade*. Then show youngsters the book *The Scarecrow's Hat* by Ken Brown and tell them there is a word in the story that means the same as *trade*. Read the story aloud. Then challenge students to name the mystery word (swap). *Vocabulary*
Thursday Number a supply of corn cutouts (pattern on page 69) from 1 to 12. Display a large cornstalk cutout and distribute the corn to student volunteers. Have the youngsters sequence the corn cutouts on the stalk, beginning with 1 at the bottom of the stalk, and ending with 12 at the top. Then have students count backwards from 12 as you "pick" the corn. *Number order* 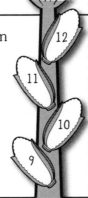	Revisit yesterday's story. Then complete "Trading Treasures" on page 62. *Recalling events*
Friday Invite students to sit in a circle and pretend to be hungry crows. Play a recording of music and have students pass a corn cutout (pattern on page 69). After a few moments, stop the recording and say, "Boo!" The child holding the corn moves to the center of the circle and becomes the scarecrow. Play continues as described, replacing the scarecrow each time. For added fun, invite the scarecrow to join you in saying, "Boo!" *Participating in a game*	**Smiling Scarecrow** *(See directions on page 62.)* 

Literacy and Math

Announce a pair of words. Ask the students whether the words rhyme. If the word pair rhymes, draw a part of the scarecrow's body on the board. If the words do not rhyme, do nothing to the scarecrow drawing and announce another word pair. Continue until the scarecrow's entire body is drawn. ***Rhyming words***

Give each pair of students several cutout copies of the corn pattern on page 69. Have one child in each twosome lie on the floor as his partner arranges corn end to end to measure his height. Have partners switch places and repeat the activity. ***Nonstandard measurement***

Color and cut out several copies of the large crow pattern on page 64. On the board, draw a large scarecrow with extra long arms labeled as shown. Announce a word and have students clap the syllables. Invite volunteers to post a crow on the corresponding arm. ***Counting syllables***

Draw a large scarecrow on a board and write letters in random order on the scarecrow's clothes. Invite a student to name a letter and place a sticky note patch over the letter. Continue until each letter has been covered. ***Letter identification***

Randomly arrange a set of number cards in a pocket chart. Secretly hide a copy of the small crow pattern on page 64 behind a number card. Ask a student to identify a number and look behind the corresponding card for the crow. When the crow is revealed, invite youngsters to scare him away by shouting, "Boo!" Then have students close their eyes as you hide the crow for another round. ***Number identification***

Song

(sung to the tune of "Daisy, Daisy")

Scarecrow, Scarecrow,
Show me what you can do!
Flap your arms. Boo!
Scare off a crow or two!
Just wiggle and wave and sway.
You'll keep those crows away
So they won't eat
The corn so sweet.
No one else can scare crows like you!

Phonological awareness: Guide students to notice the rhyming pairs throughout the song.

Journal Prompts

- Write and complete the following sentence: A scarecrow's job is… Illustrate your sentence.

- Draw a scarecrow with crows sitting on its arms. Write about it.

- Write and complete the following sentence: The scarecrow looks ____. Illustrate your sentence.

- Write and complete the following sentence: The best way to scare a crow is… Illustrate your sentence.

- Write and complete the following sentence: If I were a scarecrow… Illustrate your sentence.

Trading Treasures

Getting ready: Cut out a copy of the picture cards on page 64 and obtain a straw hat.

Steps:

1. Place the picture cards in the hat.
2. Have a volunteer take a card and name the item on the card. Then have another student name the animal that wants the item and tell why. (See Wednesday's read-aloud on page 60.)
3. Continue until no cards remain in the hat.
4. If desired, return the cards to the hat and play again. This time have students name the animal that trades the item for another item.

Smiling Scarecrow

Materials for one scarecrow: paper plate cut as shown, 6" tan circle, thin yellow paper strips, 9" x 12" sheet of light blue construction paper, crayons, scissors, glue

Steps:

1. Draw a face on the circle and glue it in the middle of the blue paper.
2. Cut the yellow strips (hay) to fit around the scarecrow's face. Glue in place.
3. Color both sides of the paper plate and glue it above the scarecrow's face, as shown, to create a hat.
4. Use crayons to add desired clothing.

TEC61176

Picture Cards and Crow Patterns

Use with the "Scarecrows" unit on pages 59–62.

TEC61176

TEC61176

TEC61176

TEC61176

TEC61176

TEC61176

TEC61176

TEC61176

TEC61176

Day-by-Day Kindergarten Plans • ©The Mailbox® Books • TEC61176

Fall Harvest

Centers for the Week

ABC Center: Program each of 26 apple cutouts with a letter from *A* to *Z*. Randomly spread out the apples on a large tree cutout. A student "picks" the apples from the tree in order. ***ABC order***

Reading Center: Write high-frequency words on a supply of potato cutouts and then laminate the potatoes. Bury the potatoes in a tub of sand or rice. A student uses a plastic shovel to dig up each potato. Then he reads the word on the potato. ***High-frequency words***

Math Center: Gather two small baskets and a supply of apple and pumpkin cutouts. A student rolls a die or a number cube and then puts a corresponding number of apples in a basket. He repeats this process with the pumpkins. Then he counts and compares the amount in each basket. ***Comparing sets***

Fine-Motor Center: Scatter assorted-size orange pom-poms (pumpkins) on a large sheet of green construction paper (pumpkin patch). A student uses a clothespin to "pick" the pumpkins and put them in a small basket. ***Pincer grasp***

Science Center: Set out magnifying glasses, a balance scale, counting bears, lengths of yarn, and a supply of fall fruits and vegetables, such as apples, miniature pumpkins, and potatoes. A student observes, measures, and compares the fruits and vegetables using the materials at the center. ***Observation***

Morning Group Time	Read-Alouds and Art
Monday Place on the floor a large sheet of brown paper (field) and a supply of potato cutouts. Show students one of the potatoes. Ask them to estimate how many potatoes will fit in the field without overlapping. Write each child's name and estimate on the board. Have students keep count as you fill the field with potatoes. Then help students compare the total with the estimates. *Estimation*	Read aloud *Fall Harvest* by Gail Saunders-Smith. Ask students to discuss why some foods are harvested by people and some are harvested by machines. Then invite students to discuss which harvesting method they think would be easier and tell why. *Supporting an opinion*

Monday

Place on the floor a large sheet of brown paper (field) and a supply of potato cutouts. Show students one of the potatoes. Ask them to estimate how many potatoes will fit in the field without overlapping. Write each child's name and estimate on the board. Have students keep count as you fill the field with potatoes. Then help students compare the total with the estimates. *Estimation*

Read aloud *Fall Harvest* by Gail Saunders-Smith. Ask students to discuss why some foods are harvested by people and some are harvested by machines. Then invite students to discuss which harvesting method they think would be easier and tell why. *Supporting an opinion*

Tuesday

Set out a variety of fall fruits and vegetables. Announce clues about a chosen food. Invite volunteers to name the described food. Once the answer is revealed, repeat the activity for the remaining foods. *Critical thinking*

Harvest Soup
(See directions on page 68.)

Wednesday

Show students a pear and a pumpkin. Draw a T chart on the board and label it as shown. Encourage students to name likenesses and differences as you write their responses on the chart. *Making comparisons*

Alike	Different

Read aloud *The Enormous Potato* by Aubrey Davis. Ask students to pretend they are the farmer. Invite them to share what they would do with the potato. *Responding to literature*

Thursday

Write a message about a variety of fall fruits and vegetables, leaving extra space between each line. Read the message with students. Invite volunteers to locate the name of a fruit or vegetable and then draw a corresponding illustration above the name. *Matching pictures to print*

Revisit yesterday's story to review the sequence of events. Guide a group of students to reenact the story while their classmates are the audience. Continue as described so each student gets a turn to reenact a part of the story. *Retell a story*

Friday

Ask students what mashed potatoes, fries, and potato chips have in common. After students announce that all three foods are made from potatoes, help youngsters make a graph to show their potato preferences. *Graphing*

Corny Decorations
(See directions on page 68.)

Literacy and Math

Place a set of magnetic letters in a bag. Cut out a class supply of the corn pattern on page 69. Program each cutout with several different letters. Give each child a cutout and access to colorful bingo daubers. To play, remove a letter from the bag and place it on a magnetic board. Each child who has the letter on his corn marks the letter with a dauber. Continue until all the letters have been called. *Letter matching*

Make a copy of the cards on page 69 and cut off the number on each card. (Discard the numbers.) Then make enough copies of the cards for each child to have five cards. Have each child spread out her cards faceup. Write a number from 1 to 10 on the board. Have a volunteer identify the number. If a child has a card with that many pears, she turns it over. Erase the board and write a different number to continue. *Counting*

On a supply of sentence strips, write simple rebus sentences naming fall foods and their colors. Cut each sentence to remove the color word. Display the sentences and words separately in a pocket chart. Help a volunteer read aloud the words on a strip and then move the corresponding color word to finish the sentence. Next, have students read the sentence aloud. *Reading color words*

The pumpkin is | orange.

Have each child cut out a copy of the cards on page 69 and stack them facedown in front of him. Pair students. At the same time, each partner turns over his top card. The partners compare their numbers and determine which number is larger. They continue for each remaining card. *Comparing numbers*

Tell students that popcorn is one of the oldest types of corn and it has small, hard kernels unlike an ordinary ear of corn. Show students some popcorn kernels and some popped popcorn. Then give each child a sheet of paper and have him write and illustrate a sentence to describe the popcorn. *Writing*

Popcorn is white and yummy.

Song

(sung to the tune of "O Christmas Tree")

It's harvesttime! It's harvesttime!
The garden's full of veggies.
It's harvesttime! It's harvesttime!
The garden's full of veggies.
Beans, corn, and squash are growing there.
So many tasty things to share.
It's harvesttime! It's harvesttime!
The garden's full of veggies.

Phonological awareness: Invite students to name words that begin with /h/ like *harvest*.

Journal Prompts

- Draw a yellow fall fruit or vegetable. Write about it.

- Write and complete the following sentence: If I worked at a farmers' market, I would want to sell _____.

- Draw a fall fruit or vegetable that is small. Write about it.

- Draw a fall fruit or vegetable that is big. Write about it.

- Write and complete the following sentence: My favorite fall food is _____. Illustrate your sentence.

Instructions

Harvest Soup

Materials for one project: colorful construction paper scraps, piece of orange tissue paper, disposable bowl, plastic spoon, scissors, glue

Steps:
1. Glue the spoon near the inside edge of the bowl.
2. Crumple the tissue paper and glue it inside the bowl.
3. Cut paper scraps so they resemble fall vegetables. Glue the veggies on the tissue paper.

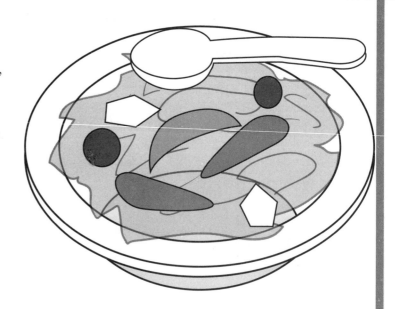

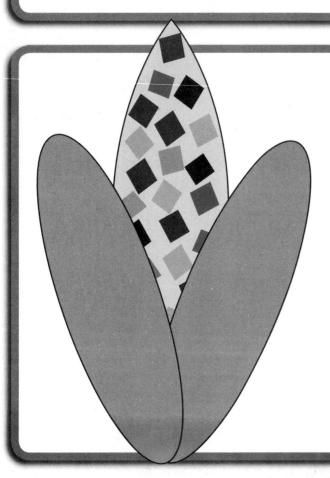

Corny Decorations

Materials for one project: 2½" x 8" piece of yellow paper; two 6" green paper ovals; thin paper strips in the following colors: brown, orange, red, and purple; scissors; glue

Steps:
1. To make a husk, glue one end of each green oval together, keeping the other ends spread apart.
2. Glue the husk to one end of the yellow rectangle (corn). Trim the two corners on the end of the corn opposite the husk.
3. Cut the paper strips into small pieces (kernels).
4. Glue the kernels on the corn.

1		6	
2		7	
3		8	
4		9	
5		10	

TEC61176

Corn Pattern
Use with the "Scarecrow" unit on pages 59–62 and the "Fall Harvest" unit on pages 65–68.

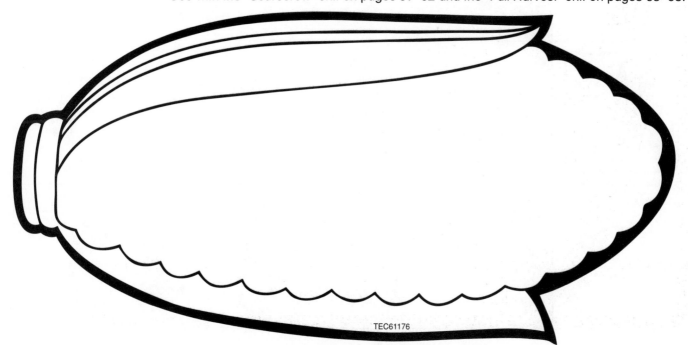

TEC61176

Harvesttime

Say the name of the first picture in the row.
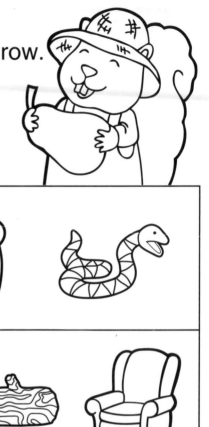 Color the rhyming pictures in the row.

Day-by-Day Kindergarten Plans •©The Mailbox® Books • TEC61176

Thanksgiving

Centers for the Week

Reading Center: Set out pictures to represent one- and two-syllable words along with a large corn cutout and a large turkey cutout. A student counts the syllables in each word and places the pictures of one-syllable words on the corn and the pictures of two-syllable words on the turkey. ***Phonological awareness***

Writing Center: Provide turkey body cutouts programmed with "I am thankful for…" Also provide a large supply of feather cutouts. On each of several feathers a student writes and draws something for which she is thankful. Then she attaches the feathers to the turkey's body. ***Writing***

Math Center: Program each of ten paper plates with a different dot set. Program turkey leg cutouts with the corresponding numbers. Place the plates and cutouts at a center. A student matches each drumstick to the appropriate plate. ***Matching numbers to sets***

Fine-Motor Center: Set out play dough scented with pumpkin pie spice, along with toy rolling pins, disposable pie pans, and plastic knives. A student rolls and shapes the play dough to make pumpkin pies. ***Building hand strength***

Game Center: Cut apart a copy of the food cards on page 75. Stack the cards facedown and set out four plates. Each player takes a card and puts it on his plate. The students continue drawing cards, with each child placing the card on his plate if he doesn't have one like it and returning it to the bottom of the stack if he does. ***Taking turns***

	Morning Group Time	Read-Alouds and Art
Monday	Play a game of Turkey, Turkey, Pilgrim following the rules of Duck, Duck, Goose. When a Pilgrim catches a turkey, everyone in the circle says, "Gobble, gobble." Then the turkey finds a seat in the circle and the Pilgrim becomes the turkey during the next round. ***Participating in a game***	Pair students and invite each child to tell her partner whether she celebrates Thanksgiving and, if she does, how she celebrates the holiday. Then read aloud *The Perfect Thanksgiving* by Eileen Spinelli. ***Prior knowledge***
Tuesday	Label a class supply of seed cutouts with high-frequency words and scatter the seeds faceup on the floor. Play a recording of music and invite students to trot like turkeys around the seeds. Stop the recording and instruct each turkey to pick up a seed. Then help each child read his word. ***High-frequency words***	Revisit the illustrations of the hand turkey in yesterday's book. Have each student make a hand turkey. (See directions on page 74.) Collect the turkeys and place them around the room. Have each student find his turkey and use positional words to describe its location. ***Positional words***
Wednesday	Have students sit in a circle. Then give each child a personalized pumpkin cutout. Pass a disposable pie plate to a student. Instruct her to state something for which she is thankful. Then have her put her pumpkin in the plate and pass the plate to the next student. Continue until every student has had a turn. ***Oral language***	Read aloud *'Twas the Night Before Thanksgiving* by Dav Pilkey. Give each student a sheet of paper and tell him to imagine he saved a turkey. Instruct him to write about and illustrate the plans he and his turkey have for Thanksgiving. Collect the pages and bind them together to make a class book. ***Creative writing***
Thursday	On chart paper write a Thanksgiving story starter, such as "One cold November morning, Tom Turkey realized Thanksgiving would be here soon." Invite students to dictate sentences to complete the story. When the story is finished, read it aloud with students. ***Shared writing***	Read aloud *A Turkey for Thanksgiving* by Eve Bunting. Turkey tries to hide in his nest but is easily found by Mr. Moose. Give each student a sheet of paper and have her draw a better hiding place for Turkey. Invite her to share her drawing. ***Making connections***
Friday	Post a large turkey cutout without feathers. Give each child a feather cutout. Instruct him to draw at the top of his feather something that begins with /t/ as in *turkey*. Have him share his drawing and then attach the feather to the turkey. ***Beginning sound /t/***	**Paper Plate Turkey** *(See directions on page 74.)*

Literacy and Math

Cut a supply of same-size turkey feathers. Give each student a few feathers and instruct her to use the feathers to measure the lengths of different objects in the room. **Nonstandard measurement**

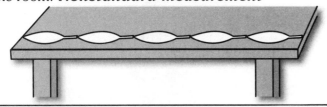

Randomly arrange a set of letter cards in a pocket chart. Secretly hide a small turkey cutout behind a card. Have a student identify a letter and look behind the corresponding card for the turkey. Encourage students to continue until they find the turkey. **Letter identification**

Label each of three large nest cutouts with a different letter. Program a supply of turkey cutouts with clip art pictures or stickers that begin with the corresponding letters. Place the nests on the floor and put the turkeys around the nests. Invite a student to take a turkey, say the name of the picture, and then place the turkey on the appropriate nest. Continue in the same way for each remaining turkey. **Beginning sounds**

Give each student a simple turkey cutout without feathers and a supply of colorful paper strips (feathers). Display a number and instruct students to place the corresponding number of feathers on their turkeys. Have students remove the feathers. Then continue using different numbers. **Making sets**

6

Have each child draw on a paper plate the foods she would like to eat for Thanksgiving dinner. Instruct her to glue her plate to a sheet of construction paper and then write a sentence about her food choices. **Writing**

Song

(sung to the tune of "Five Little Ducks")

Let's celebrate Thanksgiving Day.
It's such a special holiday.
All the family's here
And the table's neat.
We say our thank yous and it's time
     to eat.
Eat, eat, eat!
Eat, eat, eat!
We say our thank yous and it's time
     to eat!

Letter recognition: Display the song. Then invite youngsters to circle the *t*'s in the song.

Journal Prompts

- Write and complete the following sentence: The turkey is… Illustrate your sentence.

- Write and complete the following sentence: On Thanksgiving my family… Illustrate your sentence.

- Draw yourself eating your favorite Thanksgiving food. Write about it.

- Draw a Pilgrim. Write a fact about Pilgrims.

- Draw a Native American. Write a fact about Native Americans.

Hand Turkey

Materials for one turkey: white construction paper, scissors, crayons

Steps:

1. Trace your hand on the paper.
2. Color each of the four fingers of the tracing a different color. Color the rest of the tracing brown.
3. Use crayons to draw the eyes, a beak, a wattle, the legs, and other desired details.
4. Cut out your turkey.

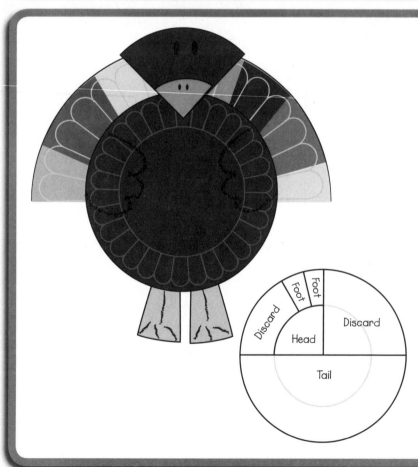

Paper Plate Turkey

Materials for one turkey: large paper plate divided as shown, small paper plate, crayons, scissors, glue

Steps:

1. Cut the divided plate on the lines and discard the extra pieces.
2. Color the feet, head, and tail.
3. Color the back of the small paper plate (body) brown. Draw wings on the body.
4. Glue the small plate to the tail.
5. Glue the head and feet to the project as shown.

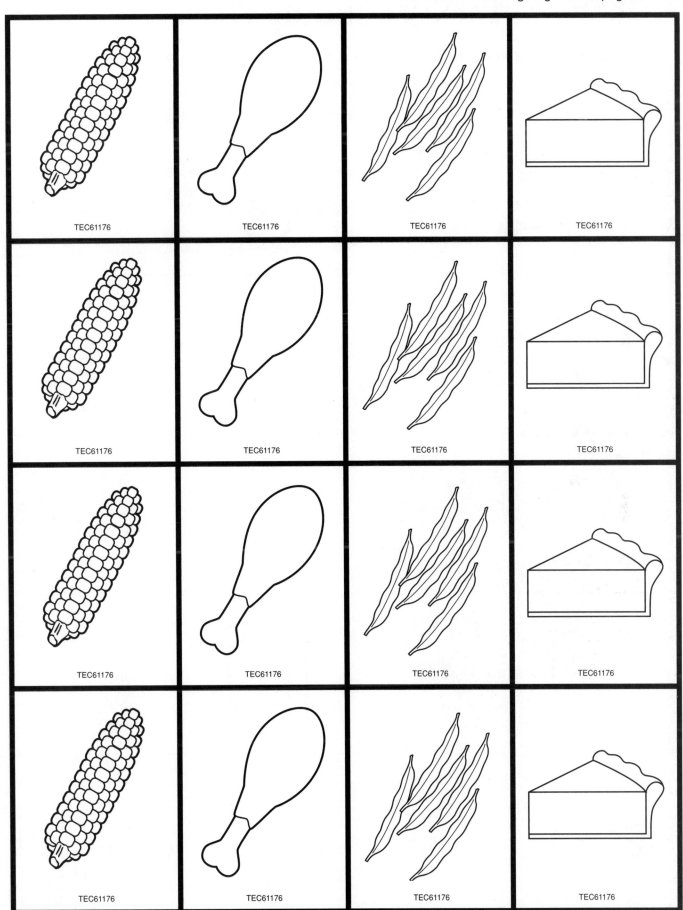

TEC61176   TEC61176   TEC61176   TEC61176

TEC61176   TEC61176   TEC61176   TEC61176

TEC61176   TEC61176   TEC61176   TEC61176

TEC61176   TEC61176   TEC61176   TEC61176

Turkey's Hiding Place

Help Turkey hide.

Color each picture that that starts like .

Bears

Centers for the Week

ABC Center: Set out a large and small bear cutout. (Use the patterns on page 81, enlarging or reducing as needed.) Also set out a supply of uppercase and lowercase *b* cards. A student puts the uppercase letters on the large bear and the lowercase letters on the small bear. ***Uppercase and lowercase letters***

Reading Center: Write on two different sentence strips "Bears eat honey, berries, and fish." Post one sentence strip and cut apart the words on the second strip. A student manipulates the words to match the posted sentence. Then on her paper she copies the sentence and illustrates it. ***Making sentences***

Writing Center: On a paper plate, squirt honey to make an uppercase and a lowercase letter *b*. A student uses bear-shaped crackers to trace the letters on her plate before eating the crackers. Then she writes the letters several times on a sheet of paper. ***Letter formation***

Math Center: On each of 20 fish cutouts, write a different number from 1 to 20. Spread the fish on a construction paper river cutout. A student dons a personalized bear headband and then "catches" the fish. Then he puts the fish in order. ***Number order***

Fine-Motor Center: Provide tagboard bear tracers, brown paper bags, and a variety of craft materials. A student traces a bear on a bag and cuts out the tracing. Then she uses the craft materials to decorate her bear. ***Tracing, cutting***

Morning Group Time	Read-Alouds and Art
Monday Attach a bear cutout (pattern on page 81) to a craft stick. On chart paper, write a message about bears. As you read the message with students, point to each word with the bear pointer. Then invite volunteers to use the bear pointer to point to the *b*'s found in the message. ***Letter identification***	Give each student a sheet of paper and invite him to draw something he does every night before he goes to bed. Allow students to share their drawings. Then read aloud *Good Night, Baby Bear* by Frank Asch. ***Text-to-self connections***
Tuesday Ask each student to bring a teddy bear to school. (Have extra bears on hand.) Direct students to group the bears by attributes, such as size, color, or clothing. ***Sorting*** 	Revisit yesterday's story. Have each student draw on separate index cards the following pictures: an apple, leaves with dripping water, a moon, and Baby Bear hugging Mother Bear. Instruct students to arrange the cards to show the order Baby Bear needs these things in the story. ***Sequencing events***
Wednesday Instruct a student to name a word that begins like *bear* and then put her head down and pretend to sleep. Continue in this manner until all the students are sleeping. Then announce, "Spring is here!" At this time, the students stand up and stretch like bears waking from a long nap. ***Beginning sounds***	**Bookmark Bear** *(See directions on page 80.)*
Thursday Tape a five-foot-tall section of black bulletin board paper to a classroom wall. Explain that the average height of a black bear is five feet. Use a white crayon to mark each child's height on the strip. Then direct students to compare their heights to the height of a black bear. ***Investigating living things***	Show students the inside cover of *Bear Wants More* by Karma Wilson. Guide them to discuss that it is spring and soon Bear will be awake. Invite students to predict what Bear wants to do when he wakes. Then read aloud the story. ***Making predictions***
Friday Set out a large box (cave) and several stuffed bears in different colors and sizes. Instruct students to cover their eyes. Then move one or two bears to the cave to hibernate. Have students open their eyes and describe the missing bear or bears. ***Visual memory, descriptive words***	**Square Bear** *(See directions on page 80.)* 

Literacy and Math

Make five colorful bear cutouts using the pattern on page 81 and draw a mountain on your board. Sing the song below and have a student move the appropriate bear over the mountain. Repeat the song, changing the ordinal number and color word each time. **Ordinal numbers**

(sung to the tune of "The Bear Went Over the Mountain")

The [first] bear over the mountain, *(Repeat two more times.)*
Was the [yellow] bear.

Post a photograph of a grizzly bear and a photograph of a black bear. On your board, draw a Venn diagram. Have students describe the bears. Discuss students' responses and write them in the appropriate areas of the diagram. **Using a graphic organizer**

Give each student a copy of the math mat on page 82 and 20 fish-shaped crackers. Write a number on the board and instruct her to "feed" the bear the appropriate number of fish. Continue as described using different numbers. **Making sets**

Announce a word. If the word ends like *bear,* the students roar like a bear. If the word ends differently, the students sit quietly. Repeat the process with several words. **Ending sounds**

Label separate blueberry cutouts with a different number from 1 to 20. Draw a large bush outline on your board and randomly post the blueberries inside the outline. Invite your little bears to "pick" the blueberries in order and post them below the bush. **Number order**

Song

(sung to the tune of "For He's a Jolly Good Fellow")

The bear gets ready for winter.
The bear gets ready for winter.
The bear gets ready for winter.
It's getting cold outside!
She finds a warm place to hide
And snuggles asleep inside!
The bear gets ready for winter.
The bear gets ready for winter.
The bear gets ready for winter.
It's getting cold outside!

Word recognition: Display a copy of the song. Tell students that the sight word *for* is in the song six times. Invite volunteers to circle the word each time it appears.

Journal Prompts

- Write and complete the following sentence: Bears are_____. Illustrate your sentence.

- Write and complete the following sentence: A bear's favorite food is _____. Illustrate your sentence.

- Would you like to hibernate like a bear? Why? Write a response and illustrate it.

- Draw your favorite kind of bear. Write about it.

- What would you do if you met a talking bear? Write a response and illustrate it.

Instructions

Bookmark Bear

Materials for one bookmark: large craft stick labeled as shown, large light brown pom-pom, 3 small dark brown pom-poms, 1 miniature black pom-pom, black permanent marker, craft glue

Steps:

1. Glue the large pom-pom to the top of the craft stick.
2. Glue the three small pom-poms to the large one to make the bear's ears and muzzle.
3. Glue the miniature pom-pom (nose) to the muzzle.
4. Use the marker to draw two small black eyes on the bear.

"Bear-y" Good Reader

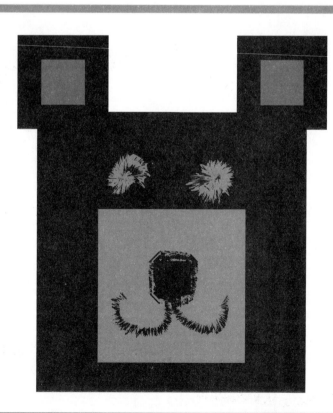

Square Bear

Materials for one bear: 9" black paper square (head), two 3" black paper squares (ears), two 1½" brown paper squares (inner ears), 5" brown paper square (muzzle), crayons, glue

Steps:

1. Glue the ears to the head. Then glue an inner ear to each ear.
2. Glue the muzzle to the bear's head.
3. Use crayons to add eyes, a nose, and a mouth to the bear.

Name

Feed Me!

Day-by-Day Kindergarten Plans • ©The Mailbox® Books • TEC61176

Note to the teacher: Use with the "Bears" unit on pages 77–80.

Happy Holidays

Centers for the Week

ABC Center: Program pairs of foam latke cutouts with corresponding uppercase and lowercase letters. A student spreads out the latkes facedown on a cookie sheet. Then she uses a plastic spatula to flip over two latkes at a time to look for matches. *Matching uppercase and lowercase letters*

Reading Center: Label each of three stars with a different rime and place each star at the top of a separate evergreen tree cutout. Program a supply of round ornament cutouts with corresponding words. A student reads each word and places it on the appropriate tree. *Word families*

Math Center: Set out a gift box containing random numbers of small holiday-related items, such as candles, gift bows, wrapped candy canes, and jumbo jingle bells. A student sorts the objects. *Sorting*

Fine-Motor Center: Provide wrapping paper, scissors, tape, ribbon, and assorted gift boxes. A student selects a box and uses the supplied materials to wrap the box. *Folding, cutting*

Game Center: Secure a large stocking cutout to the floor. Set a supply of beanbags several feet away. A student tosses beanbags, attempting to make them land on the stocking. *Gross-motor skills*

	Morning Group Time	Read-Alouds and Art
Monday	Attach a small gift bow to a craft stick to make a pointer. Write on the board a message about the upcoming holidays. Invite students to use the pointer to identify first and last words in a sentence, uppercase and lowercase letters, ending punctuation, and high-frequency words. ***Print concepts*** 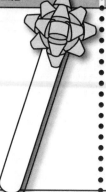	Share the cover of *Messy Bessey's Holidays* by Patricia and Fredrick McKissack. Point out the cookies and ask students which cookies Bessey makes for each holiday. Invite volunteers to name other cookie shapes Bessey could make. Then read the book aloud. ***Prior knowledge***
Tuesday	Invite students to name different holiday greetings, such as "Merry Christmas," "Happy Hanukkah," and "Happy Kwanzaa." Then have each student complete the "Cards for Friends" activity on page 86. ***Writing***	Revisit the section of yesterday's book when Bessey delivers her cookies. Invite students to study the illustrations on these pages. Ask volunteers to tell how Bessie knows to which house to deliver each type of holiday cookie. ***Making connections***
Wednesday	Have students sit in a circle and discuss the Kwanzaa principle of *Kujichagulia* (self-determination). Pass a candle or a candle cutout to a student. Have her state a goal she has set for herself and pass the candle to the next student. Continue as described until each student has stated a goal. ***Holiday customs***	Read aloud *The Mouse Before Christmas* by Michael Garland. Stop the story when Mouse begins his trip on Santa's sleigh. Pair students and invite each partner to tell the other what he thinks Mouse will see on his journey. Finish reading the story. ***Making predictions***
Thursday	Cut apart several copies of the holiday cards on page 87. Seat youngsters in a circle. Then use the cards to create a pattern on the floor. Have volunteers add cards to extend your pattern. For an added challenge, invite students to both create and extend the patterns. ***Patterning***	In yesterday's story, the best gift Mouse receives is a new hat. Invite students to share their answers to the following question: Why did Santa give Mouse a hat just like his hat? ***Drawing conclusions***
Friday	Discuss with students that kind words are one of the best gifts. Have students sit in a circle. Give a child a wrapped gift box. Have the student give the gift to a classmate along with some kind words. The classmate repeats the process. Youngsters continue until all the students have received the gift. ***Speaking, listening***	**Holiday Centerpiece** *(See directions on page 86.)* 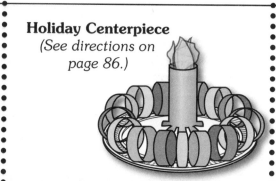

Literacy and Math

Make a copy of page 88 and write numbers on Santa's beard. Give each student a copy of the page and several cotton balls. Announce a number and have him find the number on his paper. Then instruct him to glue a cotton ball over the number. **Number recognition**

Draw a large Christmas tree outline on your board. Name a word. Have a student name a rhyming word and then draw a simple ornament on the tree. Continue in the same way until the tree is covered with ornaments. **Rhyming**

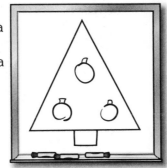

Have students use wrapped miniature candy canes to measure objects around the room. On a sheet of paper have each child draw two items she measured and the number of candy canes used to measure each item. **Nonstandard measurement**

Give a small group of students a bag of gift bows. Have a student use the bows to make a pattern. Then have the other group members read the pattern. Repeat the activity until each student has made a pattern. **Patterning**

Give each student a sheet of paper folded like a card. On the inside of the card, instruct her to draw a gift she would like to give someone and write a sentence about the gift. Have her decorate the outside of the card to resemble wrapping paper and then attach a gift bow to it. **Writing**

Song

(sung to the tune of "Twinkle, Twinkle, Little Star")

We love winter holidays, celebrating many ways.
We have all our loved ones near.
It's a family time of year.
We love winter holidays, celebrating many ways.

We love winter holidays, celebrating many ways.
Frosty days and starry nights.
Gifts and food and twinkling lights.
We love winter holidays, celebrating many ways.

Letter recognition: Display the song. Have volunteers locate and circle the *w*'s in the song. Then invite students to count the *w*'s.

Journal Prompts

- Write and complete the following sentence: My family celebrates _____. Illustrate your sentence.

- Respond to the following question: What is the best part of your family's holiday celebration? Illustrate your answer.

- Write one thing you know about Christmas. Illustrate your sentence.

- Write one thing you know about Hanukkah. Illustrate your sentence.

- Write one thing you know about Kwanzaa. Illustrate your sentence.

Instructions

Cards for Friends

Getting ready: For each child, fold a sheet of paper in half to make a card. Write each student's name on a different envelope. Give every student a card and a classmate's envelope.

Steps:
1. Decorate the outside of the card.
2. On the inside of the card, write a holiday greeting and sign your name.
3. Put the card in the envelope and deliver it to the appropriate friend.

Happy Hanukkah!
Tamera

Holiday Centerpiece

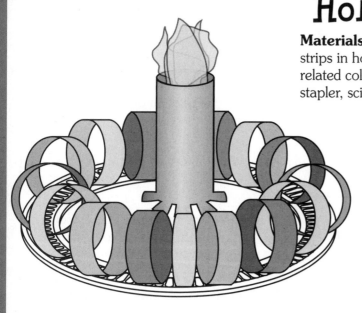

Materials for one centerpiece: fifteen 1" x 9" paper strips in holiday-related colors, square cutout in holiday-related color, orange tissue paper square, paper plate, stapler, scissors, crayons, glue

Steps:
1. Color the inside of the plate.
2. Glue each strip to form a ring. Glue each ring to the rim of the plate.
3. Roll the paper square to form a cylinder (candle) and have an adult staple the cylinder for you.
4. Glue the tissue paper into one end of the candle. Cut tabs in the opposite end of the candle as shown. Then glue the candle to the middle of the plate.

TEC61176

TEC61176

TEC61176

TEC61176

TEC61176

TEC61176

TEC61176

TEC61176

TEC61176

Name _____

Santa's Beard

Day-by-Day Kindergarten Plans • ©The Mailbox® Books • TEC61176

88   **Note to the teacher:** Use with Monday's Literacy and Math idea on page 85.

Gingerbread Pals

Centers for the Week

ABC Center: Mix ground cinnamon, cloves, and ginger into a brown-tinted batch of play dough. Set out the play dough along with a set of laminated letter cards. A child rolls the play dough into snake shapes and uses the shapes to form the letter on a card. *Letter formation*

Reading Center: Write a few simple sentences on sentence strips. Then write the words from each sentence on individual gumdrop cutouts to make sets. A child orders the gumdrops in each set to match each sentence. *Making sentences*

Math Center: Use three different-colored copies of the patterns on page 93 to make 18 gingerbread pal cutouts. A child chooses a characteristic, such as color, and sorts the pals accordingly. Then she repeats the activity using a different characteristic. *Classification*

Fine-Motor Center: Enlarge one of the patterns on page 93 to make a few gingerbread pal cutouts. For each cutout, hole-punch the perimeter and tie one end of a length of yarn to a hole. A youngster threads the yarn through the holes to create a "frosting" border. *Lacing*

Art Center: Set out cinnamon sticks, a squeeze bottle containing a mixture of white paint and glue, and gingerbread pal patterns (page 93) that have been cut from sandpaper. A child rubs the cinnamon stick on the rough side of the sandpaper. Then she adds desired details to her pal using the glue mixture. *Gluing*

Morning Group Time	Read-Alouds and Art
Monday Write the numbers from 10 to 0 on the board. Then cover all of the numbers except 10 with gingerbread pal cutouts (patterns on page 93). Invite a volunteer to point to the number 10. Then lead youngsters in counting backward from 10, removing the corresponding cutout from the board as they say each number. **Counting backward**	Read aloud *The Gingerbread Boy* by Paul Galdone. Revisit the story and discuss what happens at the beginning, middle, and end. Then help each child fold a sheet of paper into thirds. Have him draw pictures to illustrate the three parts of the story in the corresponding sections of his paper. **Beginning, middle, and end**
Tuesday Draw a large gingerbread pal on the board and program it with several high-frequency words. Also attach a gumdrop cutout to a craft stick to make a pointer. Have volunteers take turns pointing to words on the gingerbread pal and reading them aloud. **High-frequency words**	**Gingerbread Boy** *(See directions on page 92.)* 
Wednesday Prepare an equal number of gingerbread pal cutouts (patterns on page 93) and small gumdrop cutouts. Display the gingerbread pals and most of the gumdrops. (Keep a few gumdrops out of students' sight.) Ask students to predict whether there is a gumdrop for each pal. Then invite volunteers to attach a gumdrop nose to each pal. Lead students in determining how many more gumdrops are needed. Then add the remaining gumdrops. **Making predictions, one-to-one correspondence**	Read aloud *The Gingerbread Girl* by Lisa Campbell Ernst. Then revisit Monday's story. Draw a Venn diagram on the board and invite students to compare and contrast the two stories. Write each statement in the appropriate section of the Venn diagram. **Comparing and contrasting**
Thursday Prepare a supply of gingerbread pal cutouts (patterns on page 93). Hold up a large cookie sheet and one cutout. Have each child estimate the number of gingerbread pals that will fit on the cookie sheet without overlapping. Record responses on the board. Then fill the cookie sheet with gingerbread pals and lead students in counting the cookies. **Estimating**	Revisit from yesterday's story the pages with red passages indicating the Gingerbread Girl's chanting. Reread each passage and invite volunteers to identify the rhyming words. **Rhyming**
Friday Use the patterns on page 93 to make several gingerbread pal cutouts, making sure that each pal has an exact match. Display the cutouts facedown in a pocket chart. Invite students to play as in a traditional game of Concentration. **Visual memory**	**A Personalized Pal** *(See directions on page 92.)* 

Literacy and Math

Program each of 26 gingerbread pal cutouts (patterns on page 93) with a different letter. Display four cutouts with one facedown, as shown. Have students tell what letter comes next. Then flip the gingerbread pal to reveal the answer. For an added challenge, have students order all of the letters. ***Alphabetical order***

Prepare ten gingerbread pal cutouts (patterns on page 93). Place a number word card on a cookie sheet and invite a youngster to place a set of gingerbread pals on the cookie sheet to match the word. ***Number words and sets***

For this partner activity, give each pair 12 gingerbread pal cutouts (patterns on page 93). Partner 1 sorts the pals by a chosen characteristic and Partner 2 attempts to identify the sorting criterion. After Partner 2 identifies the criterion, the partners switch roles. ***Classifying and sorting***

Post of list of color words. Have each child color each gingerbread pal on a copy of page 93 a different color. Then have her cut them out and glue them to another sheet of paper, writing the corresponding color word next to each pal. ***Color words***

Label two gingerbread house cutouts, each with a different rime. Label several gingerbread pal cutouts (patterns on page 93) with corresponding word family words. Have students read each word and place the pals near the appropriate houses. ***Word families***

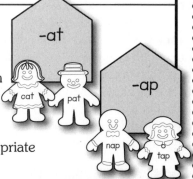

Song

(sung to the tune of "Jingle Bells")

Gingerbread cookies are such a tasty treat!
Crunchy ginger cookies—a spicy snack to eat!
Mix and roll them out, little cookie men.
Bake them, decorate them,
Eat them up, and start again!

Sequencing: Display the following props in front of the group: a mixing bowl and spoon, a rolling pin, a cookie cutter, a baking sheet, and a can of prepared frosting. Invite students to help you order the props and explain the sequence of steps for baking cookies.

Journal Prompts

- Draw a gingerbread pal cookie. Write to tell why you like or dislike gingerbread cookies.

- Draw a gingerbread pal decorated with your favorite candies. Write about your favorite candy.

- Complete the following sentence, "The gingerbread cookie ran away from..." Then illustrate your sentence.

- Draw the perfect house for a gingerbread pal. Write about the house.

- Draw your favorite kind of cookie. Write about it.

Instructions

Gingerbread Boy

Materials for one boy: newspaper strips, 4-inch brown construction paper circle, two 2" x 5" brown construction paper rectangles, lunch-size brown paper bag, scissors, crayons, glue, stapler

Steps:

1. Draw a gingerbread boy face on the circle.
2. To make feet and hands, fold both rectangles in half and trim the corners. Open each rectangle and cut on the fold.
3. Decorate the hands and feet as desired.
4. Stuff the bag with newspaper strips. Fold down the top of the bag and staple it closed.
5. Glue the pieces to the bag as shown.

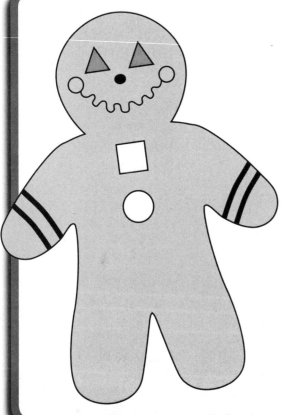

A Personalized Pal

Directions to make a glyph: Give each child a gingerbread pal cutout. Read aloud the legend provided below, pausing after each listing so students may color their cutouts. Post the completed projects with an enlarged copy of the legend. Then ask glyph-related questions for youngsters to investigate.

Legend:

Eyes: If you are a boy, draw circles for the eyes on your pal. If you are a girl, draw triangles for the eyes on your pal.

Nose: Use your favorite color to draw a nose on your pal.

Mouth: If you like pizza, add a smiling mouth to your pal. If you don't like pizza, give your pal a silly mouth.

Cheeks: If you have a pet, draw circle-shaped cheeks on your pal. If you don't have a pet, draw triangle-shaped cheeks on your pal.

Buttons: Draw a square-shaped button for each brother you have. Draw a circle-shaped button for each sister you have.

Arms and legs: If you like to read, add stripes to your pal's arms. If you like to play sports, add stripes to your pal's legs.

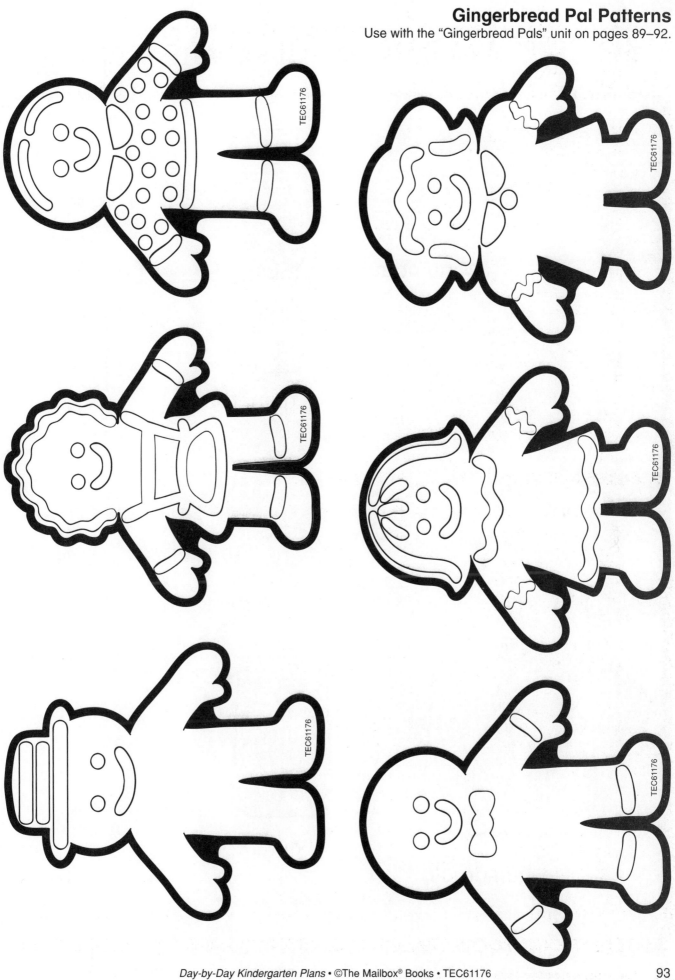

TEC61176

TEC61176

TEC61176

TEC61176

TEC61176

Fresh From the Oven

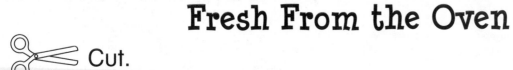

✂ Cut.
▭ Measure.
✏ Write.

_____ gumdrops

_____ gumdrops

_____ gumdrops

_____ gumdrops

_____ gumdrops

_____ gumdrops

Day-by-Day Kindergarten Plans • ©The Mailbox® Books • TEC61176

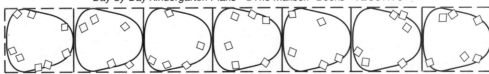

Quilts

Centers for the Week

ABC Center: A child uses a marker to write an uppercase or lowercase *q* in each square on a copy of page 99. Then she lightly colors the squares with crayons to make a *q* quilt. ***Letter formation***

Writing Center: Post a prompt such as "When I'm under a cozy quilt, I like to…" Also place at the center a cozy quilt. For inspiration each student covers her legs with the quilt and then writes or dictates her response to the prompt. Then she adds an illustration. ***Written expression***

Math Center: Set out a variety of patterned and solid-colored paper squares. A youngster glues squares onto a sheet of paper to make a quilt. On a separate sheet of paper, she glues one example of each square she used. Then beside each square she writes how many of those squares are in her quilt. ***Counting, number formation***

Art Center: A child arranges pattern blocks on an eight-inch white square to create a desired design. She traces around each block with the corresponding color and then colors in the shapes. ***Tracing, coloring***

Game Center: To play the partner game Tic-Tac-Quilt, set out a copy of page 99 and five 2½-inch paper squares in each of two different colors. Each player chooses a paper square color. Then they play as in a traditional game of tic-tac-toe. ***Critical thinking***

Morning Group Time	Read-Alouds and Art
Monday Spread a quilt on the floor in your group area. Have each child estimate the number of sheets of paper that will fit on the quilt without overlapping as you record his response on the board. After each youngster has made his estimate, place sheets of paper on the quilt and lead students in counting them aloud. ***Estimating***	Invite students to share what they know about quilt making. Then read aloud *The Boy and the Quilt* by Shirley Kurtz. After reading the story, lead a discussion about what students learned about quilt making from the story. ***Prior knowledge***
Tuesday Have each youngster color a copy of page 99 to make a quilt. Then name words one at a time, making sure that some start with the sound of *q*. If a word begins with the sound of *q*, each child holds up her quilt. If it does not, she keeps her quilt in her lap. ***Beginning sound of q***	Revisit yesterday's story. Have each child design and draw a quilt she would like to have. Then have her write a sentence describing her quilt. ***Written expression***  I would make a crazy quilt with lots of colors.
Wednesday Program the backs of pairs of patterned-paper squares with matching uppercase and lowercase letters. Place the squares pattern side out in a pocket chart to resemble a quilt. Invite the class to play as in a traditional game of Concentration. ***Matching uppercase and lowercase letters***	Read aloud *The Quilt Story* by Tony Johnston and Tomie dePaola. In the story, the same quilt brings comfort to both girls. Invite each child to draw a picture of something that brings him comfort and then tell about his illustration. ***Making connections, oral language***
Thursday Pose a question about quilts, such as "Do you have a quilt in your home?" Then help your youngsters use name cards to make a graph in a pocket chart using cards labeled "Yes" and "No" as column headers. ***Graphing***	After rereading yesterday's story, ask students to name the different things that Abigail uses her quilt for. Then challenge students to think of other uses for a quilt. ***Responding to literature***
Friday On the board write a list of words that begin with the letter *q*. After reviewing the words, have each child fold a seven-inch square into quarters, open it, and then draw stitch marks along the fold lines and edges. Next, have him program the four spaces with words that begin with *q* and then glue the square onto the center of a nine-inch paper square. ***Letter-sound association*** queen | quilt / question | quick	**Crazy Quilt Square** *(See directions on page 98.)* 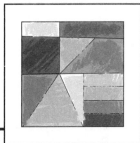

Literacy and Math

Prepare two different quilt squares. Ask students to compare and contrast the two squares as you record their responses in a Venn diagram on the board. ***Comparing and contrasting***

Remind students that many quilt blocks are made of repeated shapes. Then give each child a Geoboard and several rubber bands. Call out the name of a shape (other than a circle) and have each child create the shape on her board using only one band. Then demonstrate how to repeat the shape to make designs for a pretend quilt block. ***Shapes***

Give each child a copy of page 99. Announce a letter and have each youngster write the letter in any square on her paper. Continue with different letters until each square has a letter in it. If desired, use the resulting gameboards to play a letter lotto. ***Letter knowledge, letter formation***

Complete the activity "Alphabet Quilt". (See directions on page 98.) ***Initial consonants, alphabetical order***

Give each child a copy of page 99. Invite her to color the grid to make a quilt with an *AAB, ABB,* or *ABC* pattern. When she is finished coloring, help her write her chosen pattern at the top of the page. ***Patterning***

Song

(sung to the tune of "Are You Sleeping?")

My quilt's cozy when I'm sleeping.
I stay warm. Oh, so warm!
My teeth never chatter.
Cold air doesn't matter.
My quilt's warm, nice and warm.

Making connections: Help students make a list of things that are warm like quilts.

Journal Prompts

- Draw a quilt. Write and complete the following sentence: "Quilts are ___."

- Quilts are made of squares. Draw and write about something else that is made of squares.

- Draw a colorful quilt. Write to describe it.

- List different ways you can use a quilt.

- Pretend you have designed a magical quilt. Draw a picture of it. Then write about it.

Instructions

Crazy Quilt Square

Materials for one quilt square: 9" white paper square, 12" colorful construction paper square, ruler, black marker, crayons

Steps:
1. Divide the white paper square into sections using the ruler and the marker.
2. Use crayons to color each section of the square as desired.
3. Glue the smaller square onto the larger square.

Display the completed squares together to resemble a quilt. Then use a marker to add stitch lines along the edges of each square.

Alphabet Quilt

Materials for one alphabet quilt: 9" white paper squares, crayons, black marker

Steps:
1. Give each child a white paper square and assign her a letter from *A* to *Z.* (If needed, give some children more than one square and assign more than one letter. Or have partners work together as needed to complete the alphabet.)
2. Have each child write his assigned letter in the top left corner of his square. Then have him draw a picture of something that begins with the corresponding letter.
3. Help students work together to arrange the squares in alphabetical order to make a quilt.
4. Use the marker to add stitch marks between the quilt blocks.

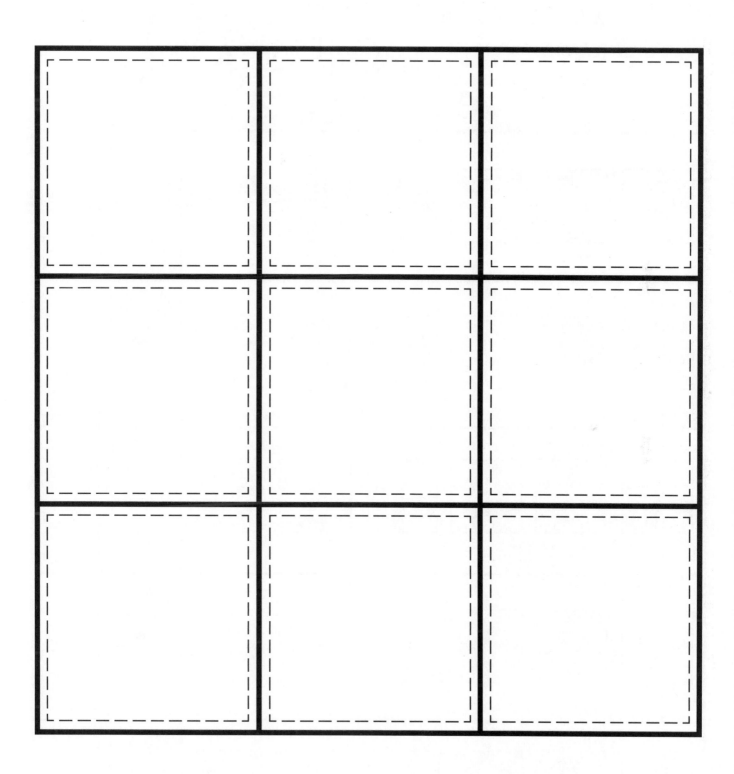

Day-by-Day Kindergarten Plans • ©The Mailbox® Books • TEC61176

Note to the teacher: Use with the "Quilts" unit on pages 95–98.

99

Patching Squares

What comes next?

Circle.

 Day-by-Day Kindergarten Plans • ©The Mailbox® Books • TEC61176

Snow and Mittens

Centers for the Week

ABC Center: Add a shallow layer of sugar to a large plastic tray so that the sugar resembles snow. Place a set of letter cards and a long carrot (snowman nose) nearby. A child chooses a card and uses the carrot to write the letter in the snow. *Letter formation*

Reading Center: Set out a pair of mitten cutouts (pattern on page 105), along with two stacks of identical high-frequency word cards. A youngster turns over a card from each stack and reads the word on each card. If the words match, she places one card on each mitten. If they do not, she returns them to the bottom of her stack. *High-frequency words*

Writing Center: A child traces a mitten shape around each of her hands on a large sheet of paper and decorates the tracings as desired. Below her drawing, she copies the sentence starter "My mittens are ____ and ____." She adds two words that describe her mittens. *Writing descriptive words*

Math Center: Draw a large snowpal without details on a sheet of poster board and place small shape cutouts nearby. A child uses desired shapes to add details to the snowpal. On a separate sheet of paper she draws one example of each shape she used. Then, beside each shape, she writes how many are on her snowpal. *Shape recognition, counting*

Art Center: A student draws an outdoor scene. Then she cuts white paper into small pieces and glues the resulting snow onto her paper to create a winter scene. *Cutting, gluing*

Morning Group Time	Read-Alouds and Art

Monday

Attach a snowflake cutout (pattern on page 105) to a craft stick to make a pointer. Write a morning message on the board. Read the message aloud, using the pointer to track the print as you read. Then ask student volunteers to use the pointer to locate punctuation marks, capital letters, high-frequency words, or other parts of the message. *Concepts of print*

Read aloud *The Snowy Day* by Ezra Jack Keats. At the end of the story, ask students to recall the different things Peter does in the snow. Then invite each child to draw a picture of her favorite thing to do in the snow and add a caption to her illustration. *Making connections*

Tuesday

Place a small amount of real snow or crushed ice in three disposable pie pans. Place a small piece of felt (blanket) over one pan, sprinkle salt on the second, and sprinkle sand on the last one. Invite students to observe the snow and determine which method causes it to melt the fastest. *Observing changes in matter*

Revisit yesterday's story. Help students use the pictures to retell the story. Then have each child make marks in snow like Peter does. (See "Making Tracks" on page 104.) *Story recall, art*

Wednesday

Program a class supply of paper snowflakes (pattern on page 105) each with a different number from 1 to 20. (Repeat numbers if needed.) Mix up the snowflakes and place them in a circle on the floor. Have students move around the flakes as they chant the verse shown. At the end of the chant, have each child pick up the snowflake he is standing closest to and identify the number. *Number identification*

Snow has fallen all around.
Pick a snowflake off the ground!

Read aloud *The Mitten* by Jan Brett. At the end of the story, Nicki's mitten stretches to hold several animals. With this activity, youngsters imagine one of their mittens houses several critters. Have each child complete the sentence starter "My mitten is so big that…" Then have her illustrate her sentence. *Responding to literature*

Thursday

Use a large foam ball (snowball) to play a version of the classic game Hot Potato called Chilly Snowball. Play a recording of music, stopping the recording periodically. Each time you stop the music, have the child holding the snowball name a word, real or nonsense, that rhymes with *snow*. *Rhyming words*

Revisit yesterday's story, reminding students that one of Nicki's mittens is much larger than the other by the end of the story. Then have each child color and cut out a copy of the mittens on page 106. Have him glue the mitten pairs in order from smallest to largest on a 12" x 18" sheet of construction paper. *Ordering by size*

Friday

Use the pattern on page 105 to make one mitten cutout for *every two* students in your class. Use a different puzzle cut on each mitten and program each half with an identical high-frequency word. Give each child a mitten half and have him find the child with the matching word. Have the two youngsters match their halves to make a mitten and read their word together. *High-frequency words*

Matching Mittens
(See directions on page 104.)

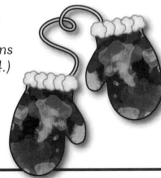

Literacy and Math

Give every two students a plastic bag containing a different number of cotton balls (snowballs). Have each twosome place the snowballs in groups of ten, returning any extras to the bag. Direct them to count by tens to determine their total number of snowballs. Then have the duos switch bags and repeat the activity. ***Counting by tens***

String a length of yarn between two chairs. Write each word from several simple sentences on an individual mitten cutout (pattern on page 105). Choose a set of mittens and clip them to the yarn out of order. Have volunteers rearrange the mittens to make a sentence. After students read the sentence aloud, remove the mittens and repeat the activity with a different set of mittens. ***Making sentences***

Play soft music as you pass a mitten containing letter manipulatives around a circle. When you stop the music, the child holding the mitten pulls out a letter, identifies it, and names a word that begins with it. ***Letter-sound association***

Have each child draw a snowpal using only one assigned shape, such as squares. Then have her count the number of the shape she used and copy and complete the sentence starter shown. ***Drawing shapes, counting***

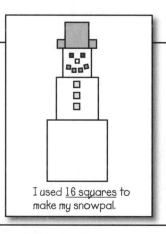

I used 16 squares to make my snowpal.

Invite each child to color and/or decorate the mittens on a copy of page 106 and cut them out. Then invite her to sort the mittens into sets as desired. Have her glue each set to a sheet of paper and write a sentence to explain her sorting criterion. ***Sorting***

Song

(sung to the tune of "I've Been Working on the Railroad")

I'll be putting on my mittens
On a snowy day!
I'll be putting on my mittens
Just to go outside and play.
I can build a frosty snowpal; cold won't bother me!
Since I'm wearing woolly mittens, I'm cozy as can be!
Mittens in the snow, mittens in the snow,
Mittens keep the cold away-ay-ay!
Mittens in the snow, mittens in the snow,
Mittens keep the cold away!

Concepts of print: Write the song on chart paper. Invite volunteers, in turn, to put on a mitten and circle the capital letters.

Journal Prompts

- Do you prefer to wear mittens or gloves? Tell why.

- Draw big and small snowflakes. Write about them.

- Mittens keep you warm in the snow. List some other things that keep you warm in the snow.

- Draw a snowpal. Write to describe it.

- Snow is cold. Draw some other things that are cold. Label each picture.

Instructions

Making Tracks

Materials for one project: "snow" (mixture of equal parts nonmenthol shaving cream and white glue), 12" x 18" sheet of black construction paper, craft stick

Steps:
1. Place a dollop of snow on your paper.
2. Use the craft stick to make lines and tracks in the snow. Write letters or numbers in the snow if desired.
3. When you're satisfied with your project, set it aside to dry.

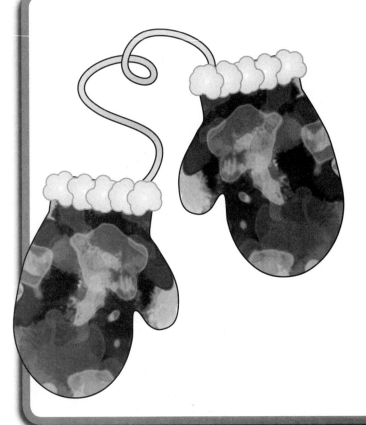

Matching Mittens

Materials for one pair of mittens: tagboard mitten tracer (pattern on page 105), cotton batting, 9" x 12" sheet of white construction paper, several colors of paint, scissors, yarn, tape, glue

Steps:
1. Fold the paper in half. Open the paper and place several dollops of colorful paint on one half of the paper.
2. Refold the paper and gently rub the surface to spread the paint. Unfold the paper.
3. When the paint is dry, refold the paper and trace the mitten on the folded paper. Cut along the resulting outline.
4. Spread glue on each mitten cuff and press cotton batting atop the glue.
5. Tape one end of a length of yarn to the back of each mitten.

Use with the "Snow and Mittens" unit on pages 101–104.

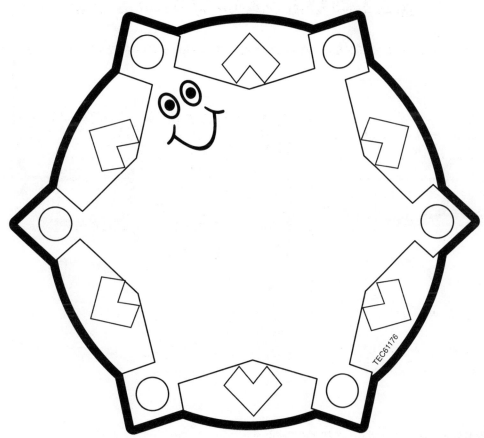

Mitten Pattern

Use with the "Snow and Mittens" unit on pages 101–104.

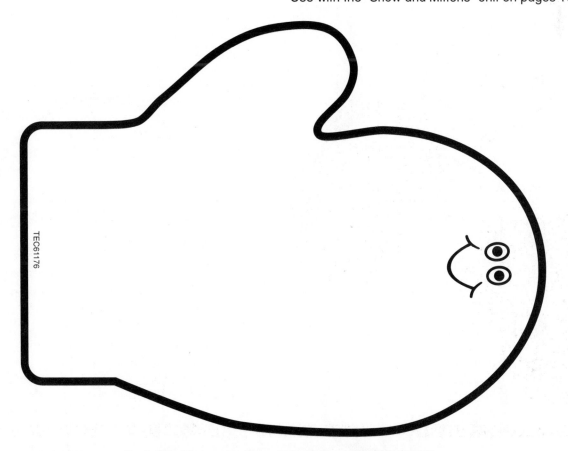

Mitten Patterns

Use with the "Snow and Mittens" unit on pages 101–104.

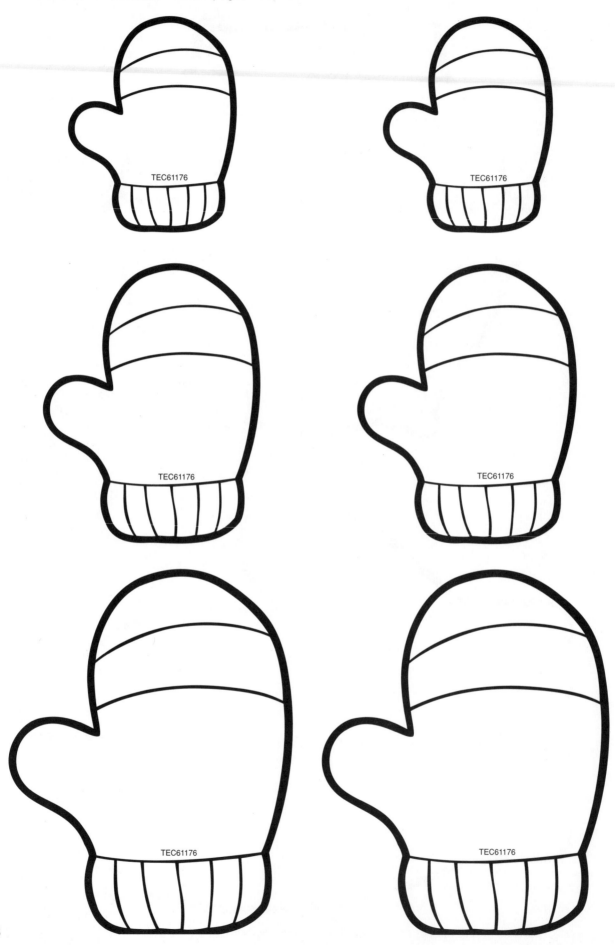

TEC61176

TEC61176

TEC61176

TEC61176

TEC61176

TEC61176

Martin Luther King Day

Centers for the Week

Reading Center: Label sentence strips "I can be a friend," scrambling the word order. A child chooses a strip and cuts the words apart. He glues them in order to a sheet of paper, with help as needed. Then he illustrates one way he can be a good friend. *Making sentences*

Art Center: Provide dove patterns (enlarge the dove on the card from page 111), white craft feathers, pieces of plastic greenery, scissors and glue. A child cuts out his dove and then glues white feathers to the cutout. Then he glues a bit of greenery to the dove's beak so the greenery resembles an olive branch. *Fine-motor skills*

Writing Center: Program a paper with a large thought cloud and the sentence starter "My dream is…" Then make a class supply and place the papers at the center. A student completes the sentence and illustrates his idea in the cloud. *Writing*

Math Center: Use the pattern cards on page 111 to make several different pattern strips. Also cut apart several extra copies of the cards. A student chooses a pattern strip and uses the cards to extend the pattern. *Patterning*

Fine-Motor Center: Provide colorful play dough and a large laminated cake cutout labeled "Happy Birthday, Dr. King!" A student uses the play dough to decorate the cake. *Squeezing*

Morning Group Time	Read-Alouds and Art

Monday

Give each child a word card labeled with *dream, peace,* or *equal.* Place in a bag a set of letter cards that match the letters in the words. Discuss the meanings of the words. Then pull out a letter card and say the letter name. Each student with a word containing the letter covers the letter with a game marker. Play continues until all the letters in the words have been covered. *Matching letters*

Read aloud *Happy Birthday, Martin Luther King* by Jean Marzollo. Then encourage students to recall facts about Dr. King and his life. Write each idea on a separate paper strip. Then attach the strips to a wall, stacking them so they resemble a tiered birthday cake. Finally, add construction paper candles to the cake. *Recalling details*

Tuesday

Announce a new class rule, such as only boys can have a snack and only girls will be able to go out to play. When students protest, ask them how the new rule makes them feel. Discuss equality and explain that Dr. King worked to make laws fair for everyone. *Understanding equality*

Peaceful Pictures
(See directions on page 110.)

Wednesday

Have students help you write a positive comment about each child on separate hand cutouts in a variety of skin tones. Then mount the handprints on your wall in a circle and add a bow to complete the friendship wreath. *Appreciating others*

Write on your board the words *hate, separate,* and *war.* Read aloud *Martin's Big Words: The Life of Dr. Martin Luther King, Jr.* by Doreen Rappaport. Then help students name the opposites of the listed words. Make the point that Dr. King didn't call the words big words because of their sizes, but because of their importance. *Opposites*

Thursday

Show students a brown egg and a white egg. Lead a discussion of what they see and how they are alike and different. Crack the eggs into two glass bowls and point out that, inside, they are just the same. Draw the connection that people may look different on the outside, but are the same inside. *Understanding differences*

Have each child color a coloring page with one crayon. On another copy of the same page, have her color one thing and then pass it to a classmate. Students continue until each child has added to the picture. Have students compare this picture to their original pages. Discuss how working together can yield unique, colorful results. *Working together, cooperation*

Friday

Give small groups of students plates with twice as many small snacks as there are people in the group. Have youngsters work together to divide the snacks evenly to be fair to every classmate in their group. Once you have checked each group's results, invite students to eat their snacks. *Equal and unequal parts*

Many Different Colors
(See directions on page 110.)

Literacy and Math

Call out addition story problems involving friends, such as the following: "There were two friends jumping rope. Three more friends joined them. How many friends were there in all?" Invite volunteers to stand in front of the group and act out the problems. Then lead the seated students to count to determine the answer. *Modeling addition*

Choose two volunteers and have the remaining students compare and contrast the students, discussing their features, likes, and dislikes. Emphasize that people are alike in certain ways and different in other ways, and that's what makes everyone interesting and unique. *Speaking*

Have each child spread frosting on a cupcake, decorate the cupcake with sprinkles, and then push a birthday candle into it. After youngsters sing a birthday song to Dr. King and eat the cupcakes, have each child color and cut out a copy of the sequence cards on page 111 and glue them to a strip of paper in the correct order. *Sequencing*

Copy a class set of the cake pattern on page 112. Invite each child to write a birthday message to Dr. King on her cake. Next, have students color, cut out, and glue their cakes to construction paper and then add desired decorations. *Writing*

Explain to students that Dr. King is known for being peaceful—he wanted to change things in America that weren't fair but he didn't want to fight or argue. He wanted to change things in a calm way. Encourage each child to share one way he can be a more peaceful person. *Speaking*

Song

(sung to the tune of "I've Been Working on the Railroad")

Let's remember Dr. King's dream
Every single day.
Let's remember Dr. King's dream.
Don't let it fade away!
He had dreams of peace and freedom
And equality.
Everyone can work together,
Including you and me!

Syllables: Display the song on chart paper. Have students clap and count the syllables of several words in the song.

Journal Prompts

- Draw something you would like to give Dr. King for his birthday. Write about it.

- Draw something you did to help a friend. Write and complete the sentence "I helped a friend _____."

- Draw something in your neighborhood or school that you would like to make better. Write about it.

- Write about one thing you would like to change in the world. Draw a picture of it.

- Draw Dr. Martin Luther King Jr. Write three things you would like to tell him.

Instructions

Peaceful Pictures

Materials for one picture: white or tan construction paper, small paint roller, black tempera paint, crayons, craft stick

Steps:

1. Color the sheet of paper, making sure big blocks of color cover the entire page.
2. Use the roller to paint over the entire page with black paint.
3. Before the paint dries, use the craft stick to draw a design or picture in the paint. The craft stick will remove the black paint and reveal the crayon colors underneath, similar to J. Brian Pinkney's illustrations in *Happy Birthday, Martin Luther King*.

Many Different Colors

Materials for one project: plastic film canisters, white construction paper, shallow pans of paint in a variety of skin tones, fine-tip markers, crayons

Steps:

1. Use the film canisters to make prints around the edge of the paper in a variety of skin tones.
2. Once the paint dries, use the markers to add facial details and hair to the circles to make children of different ethnicities.
3. Draw inside the border a picture of something you learned about Dr. Martin Luther King Jr.

TEC61176

TEC61176

TEC61176

TEC61176

Sequence Cards
Use with the "Martin Luther King Day" unit on pages 107–110.

TEC61176

TEC61176

TEC61176

TEC61176

Cake Pattern

Use with the "Martin Luther King Day" unit on pages 107–110.

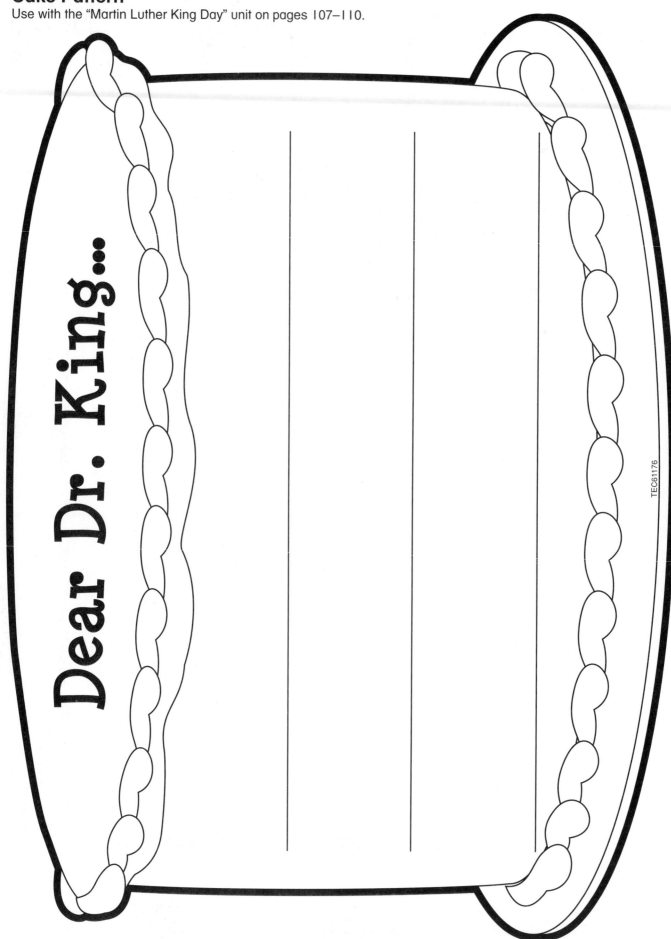

Dear Dr. King...

TEC61176

Day-by-Day Kindergarten Plans • ©The Mailbox® Books • TEC61176

Penguins

Centers for the Week

ABC Center: Use the fish pattern and picture cards on page 117 to make fish cutouts programmed with pictures. Enlarge the penguin pattern on page 117 and label it with a *p*. A student finds the fish cutouts with picture names beginning with /p/ and "feeds" them to the penguin by placing them on its tummy. *Beginning sounds*

Writing Center: Make a large two-sided copy of a penguin pattern (see page 117). Program one side with "A penguin is…" and the opposite side with "A penguin can…" and copy a class set. Provide a word bank with appropriate words and picture clues. A student uses words from the bank to complete each sentence. *Writing sentences*

Math Center: Place sheets of paper divided into sections, ink pads, and markers at a center. A student creates fish to feed to the penguins by making five fingerprints in each section on his paper; then he uses the markers to add fins and other details to each fingerprint. He then counts the fish by fives. *Counting by fives*

Science Center: Place a plastic bag in a second bag partially filled with shortening. Prepare a second set of bags without shortening. A student then slips one hand in each prop. To experience how a penguin's blubber helps it stay warm in the cold water, the child briefly submerges each hand in a container of cold water. *Investigating living things*

Game Center: Label each of 20 iceberg cutouts with a different number from 1 to 20. Attach them in numerical order to your floor. Each student pretends to be a penguin and hops from iceberg to iceberg, counting in sequence as he goes. *Number order*

Morning Group Time	Read-Alouds and Art
Monday Lead students in performing a penguin version of the song "The Hokey-Pokey," adjusting the lyrics to include students' feathered heads, beaks, right and left wings, right and left feet, and white bellies. ***Investigating living things***	Draw an iceberg shape and divide it into three sections to make a KWL chart. Have students dictate what they know and what they want to know about penguins. Then read aloud *The Emperor's Egg* by Martin Jenkins. After reading, have students dictate what they learned about penguins. ***Prior knowledge***
Tuesday Invite ten youngsters (penguins) to stand in front of the group. Lead youngsters in reciting the rhyme shown ten times, encouraging one penguin to "swim" away each time and reducing the number appropriately. ***Counting backward*** [Ten] little penguins out to play, One little penguin swims away!	Review the KWL chart from yesterday. With students standing, say several statements about penguins, some true and some false. Instruct students to waddle like penguins if the statement is true and stay still if the statement is false. ***Recalling facts***
Wednesday Choose a volunteer (penguin) to waddle away from the group and stand with his back turned and his eyes closed. Choose another penguin to leave the group to "go fishing." After that child is hidden, invite the first penguin back to guess which penguin left in search of fish. ***Visual memory***	**Penguin Parent** *(See directions on page 116.)* 
Thursday Program a penguin cutout (see page 117) with the letter *p*. Lead students in singing the song shown. Then have each child hold the penguin and name a word that begins with the /p/ sound. ***Beginning sounds*** *(sung to the tune of "I'm a Little Teapot")* I'm a little penguin, black and white. I swim in the day and I sleep at night. Penguin starts with /p/ as you can see. Name some other words that start with *p*.	Read aloud *Splash! A Penguin Counting Book* by Jonathan Chester and Kirsty Melville. Set out ten numbered penguin cutouts (see page 117) in random order. Invite volunteers to place the penguins in numerical order. Then have them practice counting backward by placing the penguins in decreasing order. ***Counting forward and backward***
Friday For each child, fill a plastic egg with beans and secure it with tape. Set a timer for one minute and challenge each student to stand still and balance the egg on his feet as if he were an emperor penguin. ***Investigating living things***	**Handy Penguin** *(See directions on page 116.)* As a follow-up activity to yesterday's book, use these penguins to create a class counting book. 

Literacy and Math

For this partner game, have each child attach a penguin cutout (see page 117) to a cup. Give each pair of students a supply of green cubes (fish). Each child rolls a pair of dice and counts the corresponding number of fish. The partners compare sets and the player who has more fish "feeds" his penguin by placing the fish in his cup.
Comparing sets

Post on the board four penguin cutouts numbered 1 to 4. Call out a penguin-related word—such as *egg*, *waddle*, or *Antarctica*—and have students clap and count the syllables. Write the word under the penguin with the corresponding number. ***Phonological awareness***

Designate one end of your classroom as the South Pole. Have youngsters (penguins) line up at the opposite end of the room. Show a different letter card to each child. Help her identify the sound the letter makes. Then encourage her to waddle ten steps toward her home. Continue playing until all penguins have found their way home. ***Letter-sound association***

For this small-group game, create a set of 12 cards with five fish drawings on each card. Have a child roll a pair of dice and take a corresponding number of cards. Lead students in reciting the rhyme shown. Then have the student count the cards by fives to determine the total number of fish. ***Counting by fives***

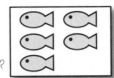

Penguin Pete likes fish, you bet!
How many fish will old Pete get?

Tell students that the largest type of penguin, the Emperor Penguin, is about four feet tall. Post a four-foot-tall penguin cutout on your wall. Invite each child to compare her height to the penguin and place an adhesive label programmed with her name on the penguin to match her height. ***Nonstandard measurement***

Poem

Five little penguins, standing on the ice.
The first one said, "This chilly weather's nice."
The second one said, "This weather is for me."
The third one said, "It's as cold as it can be!"
The fourth one said, "Let's slide across the snow."
The fifth one said, "Get ready, let's go!"
Then whoosh went the penguins all in a row
As they played in the chilly South Pole snow!

Rhyming words: Display the poem on chart paper. After students are familiar with the poem, have volunteers underline the rhyming words in each pair of lines.

Journal Prompts

- Draw a penguin. Label the parts of the penguin's body.

- Write and complete the following sentence: "If I were a penguin, _____." Illustrate your writing.

- Draw a father penguin holding an egg on his feet. Write about it.

- Draw a newly hatched penguin. Write about what he might say.

- Write and complete the following sentence: "Penguins are _____." Illustrate your writing.

Instructions

Penguin Parent

Materials for one penguin: 9" x 12" sheet of black construction paper folded into thirds with two corners trimmed as shown, white and orange heart cutouts, white oval cutout, crayons, glue, tape

Steps:

1. Draw a penguin's face on the white heart.
2. Use a white crayon to draw a penguin egg at the bottom of the center section.
3. Glue the heart cutouts and the oval cutout to the center section, making sure the oval can be lifted to reveal the egg.
4. Tape the black paper so the penguin is self-standing.

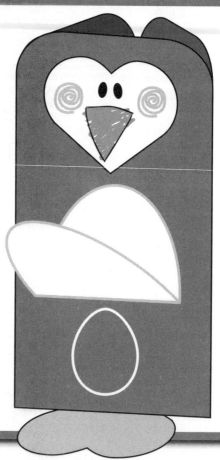

Handy Penguin

Materials for one penguin: white construction paper; red, black, and orange construction paper scraps; black paint; paintbrush; scissors; glue

Steps:

1. Make a black handprint on the white paper with the fingers positioned as shown.
2. When the handprint is dry, cut and then glue construction paper details to the project so it resembles a penguin with a bowtie.

TEC61176

TEC61176

TEC61176

TEC61176

TEC61176

TEC61176

TEC61176

TEC61176

TEC61176

TEC61176

TEC61176

TEC61176

Cool Pals

 Cut.

 Glue on the missing numbers.

2		4

	15	16

18	19	

9		11

	17	18

12		14

13	3	20	16	14	10

100th Day

Centers for the Week

Reading Center: Create and post a lined chart numbered to 100. Provide baskets of books. A student selects a book of interest, reads it to the best of his ability, and then writes the book title and his name on the chart. Youngsters continue to add to the list until the class has read 100 books. ***Reading***

Math Center: Provide ten different types of manipulatives in a bin, making sure to have ten of each type. A child sorts the manipulatives by type and then counts the groups by tens. ***Counting by tens***

Art Center: Set out a variety of small items, such as die-cut shapes, pompoms, and cereal pieces. A student counts out 100 items and creates a picture or design by gluing the items on a sheet of paper. ***Artistic expression, counting***

ABC Center: Set out metal cookie sheets and a supply of magnetic letters. A student places letters on a cookie sheet to make as many words as she can and then lists the words on a sheet of paper. Tally each child's list and challenge the class to create 100 words. ***Making words***

Game Center: Laminate several hundred charts (see page 123). Then make puzzles by cutting each chart into several pieces. For each puzzle, label the back of each piece with the same letter and place the pieces in a labeled envelope. A student selects an envelope and reassembles the chart. ***Ordering numbers***

Morning Group Time	Read-Alouds and Art
Monday Lead youngsters in making a steady beat by clapping their hands, slapping their legs, or tapping their feet. As students continue to make the beat, encourage them to count to 100 by tens. Switch to a different movement as they count to 100 by fives. Then lead students in counting by ones, switching to a new movement at the start of each set of ten. ***Counting by ones, fives, and tens***	Read aloud *One Hundred Hungry Ants* by Elinor J. Pinczes. Then have students help you connect 100 linking cubes. Reread the story, pausing to have youngsters help break the cubes into the groupings mentioned by the little ant. ***Making sets***
Tuesday Lead a class discussion about the first 100 days of school. Invite each child to recall his favorite activity or event from the first 100 days and share it aloud. ***Oral language***	Lead students in counting to 100 by tens. Then read aloud *100th Day Worries* by Margery Cuyler. After reading, have youngsters count Jessica's items by tens. Then ask students to name different items they would have brought to school to make a 100th Day collection. ***Counting by tens***
Wednesday Pass a consonant letter manipulative around your circle. Encourage each child to name a word beginning with that letter. List the words on chart paper and stop when you have listed ten words. Then pass a different letter and have the next students name ten more words. Continue until you have a list of 100 words. ***Letter-sound association***	**100 Fingers** *(See directions on page 122.)* 
Thursday Fill a large planter or window box with potting soil. Divide the class into ten small groups and have each group count out ten plant seeds. Instruct each group to plant its seeds in the planter. Place the planter in the sun and ask volunteers to water the seeds daily. ***Observing plant growth***	Read aloud *Miss Bindergarten Celebrates the 100th Day of Kindergarten* by Joseph Slate. After reading, turn back through the book and stop on each page to have volunteers identify groups of 100 items they see. ***Groups of 100***
Friday Program large blank cards by tens from 10 to 100. Give a card to each of ten students and ask them to line up in order. Have the seated children cover their eyes. Have one cardholder step aside and conceal her number. Then help the seated students count by tens to determine the missing number. ***Counting by tens***	Revisit the page in yesterday's book that shows students at a table making Heavenly 100th Day Hash. Then have each child make a helping of this tasty treat. (See directions on page 122.) ***Following directions***

Literacy and Math

Give each child a sheet of paper programmed with a picture of a pretend $100 bill and the following prompt: "If I had 100 dollars, I would _____." Instruct each child to write to complete the sentence and then illustrate his idea. **Writing**

Supply each of ten stations with different small items, such as stamps and inkpads, glue and sequins, or stickers. Have each youngster visit the stations and attach ten of each item to a construction paper strip. Once the glue is dry, staple the strip to fit her head and invite her to wear her headband. **Making sets**

Draw a hundred chart on a sheet of poster board. Cut the rows apart. Then have students reassemble the chart by sequencing the strips in a pocket chart. **Ordering numbers**

Give each pair of children a copy of a hundred chart (see page 123). Invite students to reveal a mystery design (the numeral 100) by coloring the square containing each number you call out. (See numbers list shown). **Recognizing numbers**

Numbers: 22, 60, 28, 62, 38, 72, 74, 78, 54, 56, 70, 66, 44, 46, 52, 30, 58, 40, 36, 80, 48, 24, 26, 32, 34, 42, 50, 76, 64, 68, 25, 75, 79, 29

Set a timer for 100 seconds. Then hold up a high-frequency word card and have students say the word. Continue in the same way with additional cards, having students identify as many words as they can during the 100-second time span. **High-frequency words**

the

Poem

Hooray! Hooray! Today's the day
We've all been waiting for!
We finally reached 100 days,
So let's all give a roar!
10, 20, 30, 40, 50 is halfway.
60, 70, 80, 90, 100! Hip hooray!

Counting by tens: After students are familiar with the poem, encourage them to clap as they practice counting to 100 by tens and then by fives.

Journal Prompts

- Draw how you think you might look if you were 100 years old. Write about how your life would be different.

- Write and complete the following sentence: "If I had 100 friends, I would _____." Illustrate your writing.

- Draw how you would look if you were 100 feet tall. Write about it.

- Draw how you think the world will look in 100 years. Write about it.

- Write and complete the following sentences:

  "I wish I had 100 _____.
  I'm glad I don't have 100 _____."
  Illustrate your writing.

100 Fingers

Materials for one picture:
12" x 18" sheet of light-colored construction paper, shallow pans of paint

Steps:
1. Press a hand in the paint and then make several handprints on the paper.
2. Continue with other colors of paint until you make 20 handprints.
3. When the paint is dry, count the number of fingers in your picture.

Heavenly 100th Day Hash

Getting ready: Set out ten bowls, each containing different small food items. (Suggested food items are mini pretzels, various cereals, small crackers, mini chocolate chips, gummy candies, mini M&M's candies.) Gather markers and a class supply of paper lunch sacks.

Steps:
1. Write your name on your bag. Also write the number 100 several times.
2. Take ten food items from each bowl and place them in your bag.
3. Close the bag and shake it gently to mix the ingredients.
4. Eat and enjoy!

1	2	3	4	5	6	7	8	9	10
11	12	13	14	15	16	17	18	19	20
21	22	23	24	25	26	27	28	29	30
31	32	33	34	35	36	37	38	39	40
41	42	43	44	45	46	47	48	49	50
51	52	53	54	55	56	57	58	59	60
61	62	63	64	65	66	67	68	69	70
71	72	73	74	75	76	77	78	79	80
81	82	83	84	85	86	87	88	89	90
91	92	93	94	95	96	97	98	99	100

Name _____

Plenty of Pancakes

Count by tens.  Write.

10

50

Groundhog Day and Shadows

Centers for the Week

ABC Center: Label small groundhog cutouts (see page 129) with different lowercase letters. Then label short sections of cardboard tube (groundhog burrows) with corresponding uppercase letters. A student stands each section of tube and then tucks each groundhog into the appropriate burrow. ***Uppercase and lowercase letters***

Writing Center: A student predicts whether the groundhog will see its shadow. He colors and cuts out a copy of the large groundhog pattern on page 129. Then he glues it to the top of his paper and draws a shadow or not based on his guess. He then writes a sentence to tell his prediction. ***Writing***

Math Center: Cut a strip of poster board 20 inches long (the average length of a groundhog). A student compares the length of the strip to items in the classroom, noticing items that are shorter and taller than a groundhog. ***Nonstandard measurement***

Game Center: Trace several pattern blocks onto black paper. Cut out the resulting shadows and tape them on a tabletop. Put the corresponding blocks into a cloth bag. A student reaches into the bag and feels a block. He tries to identify the matching shadow. Then he pulls out the block to check his guess. ***Sense of touch***

Science Center: Drape a large blanket over a table to create a dim cave and place several flashlights inside. A student uses the lights to experiment with shadows on the cave walls. ***Observation***

Morning Group Time	Read-Alouds and Art
Monday — Explain that some people believe if the groundhog sees its shadow on Groundhog Day, February 2, there will be about six more weeks of winter weather. Use the calendar to lead students in counting six weeks ahead. Then have them join you in counting the number of days in six weeks. ***Calendar concepts, counting***	Before Groundhog Day, read aloud *Groundhog Day!* by Gail Gibbons. Then have students predict whether they think the groundhog will see its shadow. Make a simple graph on the board to record the results. ***Predicting, graphing***
Tuesday — On a sunny morning, take students outside to a paved area. Pair students and have each youngster trace her partner's shadow with chalk and label it with an *M* for morning. Making sure the child stands in the same spot each time, repeat the activity twice more during the day, labeling the shadows *N* for noon and *A* for afternoon. Discuss why the shadows moved. ***Observation***	Read aloud *Punxsutawney Phyllis* by Susanna Leonard Hill. On the board, write the five senses as column headings. Invite students to name ways Phyllis uses her senses in the story as you list them under the headings. ***Recalling facts, five senses***
Wednesday — Lead students in a version of Simon Says by saying, "Groundhog says," and then giving them a two-step direction to follow. For example, say, "Groundhog says, 'Pop out of your burrow and turn around two times!'" and encourage youngsters to jump up quickly and turn around twice. ***Two-step directions***	**Groundhog's Shadow** *(See directions on page 128.)* 
Thursday — Place several large numbered groundhog cutouts (see page 129) in a pocket chart. Hide a groundhog shadow behind one of the cutouts. Direct a child to name one of the numbers and then look for the shadow behind the groundhog. Continue in the same way until the shadow is found. ***Number identification*** 	Read aloud *Guess Whose Shadow?* by Stephen R. Swinburne. After reading, set up an overhead projector with folders blocking the surface from students' view. Place objects on the projector one at a time, and invite volunteers to identify each object by looking at its shadow. ***Observation***
Friday — Obtain a flashlight, along with opaque objects (such as books or notebooks), translucent objects (such as waxed paper or tissue), and transparent objects (such as plastic wrap or laminating film). Have students predict which objects they think will cast a shadow. Record their predictions. Then shine the flashlight on each object and record the results. ***Making predictions***	**Shadow Art** *(See directions on page 128.)* 

Literacy and Math

Enlist students' help in creating a bank of words to describe a groundhog. Direct each child to draw a groundhog. Underneath her picture, have her write a sentence about the groundhog, using descriptive words from the word bank. **Writing a sentence, descriptive words**

My groundhog is furry and brown.

Display photos of a squirrel and a groundhog. Explain to students that the groundhog is a relative of the squirrel. Then invite them to name similarities and differences between the two animals. **Comparing and contrasting**

Take students outside on a sunny day. Lead youngsters in reciting the rhyme shown, inviting them to perform the action and observe their shadows. **Naming action words**

My shadow does what I do. Look and see!
Watch my shadow [jump] with me!

Trace a large groundhog cutout (see page 129) on black paper and cut out the resulting shadow. Pass the shadow around your circle and help each child name a word that begins with the /sh/ sound. **Digraph sh**

Select ten students (groundhogs) to sit in a line in front of the group. Recite the rhyme shown, tapping one groundhog on the shoulder during the second line and prompting him to stand up. Have a seated student use an ordinal number to name the position of the groundhog. **Ordinal numbers**

I walked by some burrows and then gave a shout,
When all of a sudden this groundhog popped out!

Song

(sung to the tune of "Pop! Goes the Weasel")

The groundhog pops up from its hole
And if it sees its shadow,
We'll all be [sad and cry, "Oh, no!"]
Six more weeks of winter!

Alternate lyrics:
[glad and shout, "Hooray!"]

Opinion: After students are familiar with the lyrics, ask them whether they prefer winter or spring. Take a class vote and adjust the lyrics if necessary before singing again.

Journal Prompts

- Draw your pretend pet groundhog. Write about it.

- Write about what else the groundhog might see when it comes out of its hole. Illustrate your writing.

- Write and complete the following sentence: "I am glad to see winter weather end because _____." Illustrate your writing.

- Write and complete the following sentence: "I am happy to see spring weather begin because _____." Illustrate your writing.

- Draw yourself coming out of a burrow. Draw your shadow. Write about what seeing your shadow might mean.

Groundhog's Shadow

Materials for one groundhog: simple groundhog and shadow cutouts, black heart cutout (nose), two red heart cutouts (ears), two white rectangle cutouts (teeth), brad fastener, markers, glue

Steps:

1. Glue the nose and ears to the groundhog.
2. Draw a mouth and other details and then glue the teeth to the mouth.
3. Attach the groundhog to its shadow with a brad.
4. Slide the cutouts to reveal the shadow.

Shadow Art

Materials for one picture: sheet of dark-colored construction paper, letter cutouts, assortment of items with interesting shapes, tape

Steps:

1. Tape to your paper letter cutouts that spell your name.
2. Place the paper in bright sunlight and arrange items around your name.
3. Leave the paper in the sun for several hours and then remove the items and the letters to reveal shadows on the paper.

TEC61176

TEC61176

TEC61176

TEC61176

Shadow Surprise!

 Write the matching lowercase letter.

L__ G__ S__ B__

J__ T__ E__ A__

R__ V__ N__ D__

Day-by-Day Kindergarten Plans • ©The Mailbox® Books • TEC61176

Valentine's Day

Centers for the Week

ABC Center: Color and cut out an enlarged construction paper copy of the heart, mailbox, and valentine patterns on page 135 and tape them to a work surface. Also cut out a copy of the picture cards on page 136. A student sorts pictures of one-syllable words onto the heart, pictures of two-syllable words onto the mailbox, and pictures of three-syllable words onto the valentine. *Phonological awareness*

Writing Center: Stock the center with colorful paper, craft materials, glue, and markers. A child creates a unique valentine for a friend. Post phrases and sentences such as "Happy Valentine's Day," "You are nice," and "I like you" for students to use in their writing. *Writing*

Reading Center: Halve several heart cutouts. Label the left halves with onsets. Label three right halves with rimes and discard the unused halves. A student puts a heart together and reads the word with help as needed. *Onsets and rimes*

Math Center: Cut out several copies of the mailbox pattern on page 135 and label each one with a different number. Label cards with corresponding sets of hearts. A child places each card on a matching mailbox. *Counting, matching sets to numbers*

Fine-Motor Center: Fill a heart-shaped candy box with brown pom-poms (candies) in three different sizes. A student uses tweezers or small tongs to remove each candy from the box and sort them by size. *Pincer grasp, sorting*

Morning Group Time	Read-Alouds and Art

Monday

Fill a large window box with potting soil. Discuss kindness with the class. As you observe acts of kindness, write each one on a heart cutout. Have each child tape his heart to a pipe cleaner stem and "plant" it in the garden. ***Promoting positive behavior***

In advance, program pairs of heart cutouts with rhyming CVC words. Read aloud *Rhyme Time Valentine* by Nancy Poydar. Then give each child a heart cutout. Help each student read his word aloud and then find the classmate with the rhyming word. ***Rhyming words***

Tuesday

Provide a supply of red, pink, white, and purple heart cutouts. Invite each youngster to choose his favorite color of heart and place it on a floor graph. Then ask questions about the resulting graph. ***Graphing***

Read aloud *Arthur's Valentine* by Marc Brown. Then have each child write a Valentine message on a strip of paper. Next, have her wrap aluminum foil around a polystyrene foam ball half so it resembles a candy kiss. Then attach the strip to the kiss. ***Writing***

Wednesday

Cut out a copy of the picture cards on page 136 and attach each one to a separate heart cutout. Place the hearts in a basket. Play music as students pass the basket. When the music stops, a child takes a heart and decides if the picture's name begins with /v/ like *valentine*. Then he returns the heart to the basket. ***Beginning sounds***

Lacy Heart
(See directions on page 134.)

Thursday

Draw ten squares (mailboxes) in a row on your board. Cut out ten hearts in different colors. Use an ordinal number to give a direction, such as "Mail the pink heart in the third mailbox." Direct a volunteer to "mail" the heart by attaching it to the corresponding mailbox. ***Ordinal numbers***

Read aloud *Chester's Way* by Kevin Henkes. On chart paper, draw a Venn diagram. Label one circle *Chester* and the remaining circle *Lilly*. Brainstorm with students unique characteristics of each character and list them in the appropriate circles. Where the circles overlap list characteristics they both share. ***Recalling facts***

Friday

Write a morning message previewing the day's events. Invite volunteers, in turn, to use a red marker to draw a heart shape around each ending punctuation mark in the message. ***Ending punctuation***

Heart Collage
(See directions on page 134.)

Literacy and Math

For this small-group game, label several valentines with money amounts of 10¢ or less. Provide penny and nickel manipulatives. Children take turns using the manipulatives to purchase valentines. **Counting pennies and nickels**

Discuss the meaning of "have a heart." Direct each child to write on a heart cutout one way she can have a heart. Have her glue her heart on red or pink paper and add decorations. Attach the hearts to a bulletin board titled "Have a Heart!" **Writing**

For this partner activity, give each child a small scoop of candy conversation hearts. Instruct each child to sort his candies by color. Next, have partners compare their sets to see who has more of each color. **Comparing sets**

Have each child use brown paper and other craft supplies to make a chocolate candy craft. Once the chocolates are made, announce words, including some that begin with /ch/. Each child holds up his chocolate piece when he hears a word that begins like *chocolate*. **Digraph ch**

For this small-group game, give each child a copy of a gameboard made up of rows of blank hearts and a die. Invite students to decorate the hearts as desired. To play, each child rolls her die and uses heart-shaped erasers (or candies) to cover a corresponding number of hearts on her gameboard. Play continues until one child covers all the hearts on her board. **Counting**

Song

(sung to the tune of "This Old Man")

Valentine's Day is here.
It's the sweetest time of year.
I'll make pretty cards
Especially for you.
I'll give hugs to my friends too!

Counting syllables: Display the song on chart paper. After students are familiar with the song, invite volunteers to draw one, two, three, or four hearts over selected words to match the number of syllables.

Journal Prompts

- Draw someone you love. Write about them.

- Draw something you would like to give your valentine. Write about it.

- Draw a friend. Write and complete the following sentence: "I like you because __."

- Draw your favorite thing to do with a friend. Write about it.

- Draw a time you did something kind for someone. Write about it.

# Instructions

Lacy Heart

Materials for one heart: large heart cutout, shallow pans of red and white tempera paint, empty thread spools, glitter

Steps:
1. Dip one end of a thread spool in paint.
2. Press the paint-covered spool repeatedly on the heart to make lacy designs.
3. Sprinkle glitter onto the wet paint.

Heart Collage

Materials for one project: sheet of white construction paper, tissue paper heart cutouts, diluted glue, paintbrush

Steps:
1. Brush a small amount of glue onto the paper.
2. Place one of the hearts on top of the glue and then brush a coat of glue over the tissue paper.
3. Repeat the process until the page is full of overlapping hearts.

Be

Mine

TEC61176

TEC61176

TEC61176

Picture Cards

Use with the "Valentine's Day" unit on pages 131–134.

TEC61176

TEC61176

TEC61176

TEC61176

TEC61176

TEC61176

TEC61176

TEC61176

TEC61176

TEC61176

TEC61176

TEC61176

TEC61176

TEC61176

TEC61176

TEC61176

Be
Mine

Teeth

Centers for the Week

ABC Center: Label a tooth cutout (see page 141) with the letter *t* and place it at the center. Gather several picture cards, making sure some of the picture names begin with /t/. A student places the pictures whose names begin with /t/ on the tooth cutout. ***Letter-sound association***

Writing Center: Set out a class supply of 2" x 12" colorful paper strips and 3" x 5" blank cards. A student writes on a strip (toothbrush handle) one way she can keep her teeth healthy. Next, she fringe-cuts the long side of a card and glues it to the handle so the project resembles a toothbrush. ***Writing***

Math Center: Label an assortment of small beanbags (pillows) with money amounts of less than ten cents. Provide a bag containing penny and nickel manipulatives. A child pretends to be the tooth fairy by counting out the corresponding amount of money and placing it under each pillow. ***Counting pennies and nickels***

Art Center: Cut a tooth shape from a sponge. A student dips the sponge in a shallow pan of white paint and makes tooth prints on a brightly colored sheet of construction paper. Before the paint dries, she sprinkles iridescent glitter on the prints. ***Artistic expression***

Game Center: For this partner game, place at a center a die, two copies of the gameboard from page 142, and two containers of 20 white Unifix cubes or other manipulatives. In turn, each child rolls the die and places on his gameboard a corresponding number of cubes. Play continues until each tooth is covered on each player's board. ***Counting***

Morning Group Time	Read-Alouds and Art
Monday	

Monday

Morning Group Time: Explain to students that both eggshells and teeth are made of calcium. Place one hard-boiled egg in a cup of water and several others in cups of brown soda. Have students predict what will happen to the shells. The next day, point out how the soda stained the eggs. Then have small groups of students use toothbrushes and toothpaste to gently clean the stained eggs. *Making observations*

Read-Alouds and Art: Program each of seven tooth cutouts (see page 141) with a different day of the week. Before reading aloud *Little Rabbit's Loose Tooth* by Lucy Bate, ask students to listen for the days of the week as they are mentioned. After reading, invite volunteers to put the tooth cutouts in order. *Days of the week*

Tuesday

Morning Group Time: Attach a tooth cutout (see page 141) to a craft stick to make a wand. Invite volunteers to use the wand to point to objects in the room that begin with /t/. *Beginning sounds*

Read-Alouds and Art: Review the story from yesterday. Then direct students' attention to Little Rabbit's ideas of what the tooth fairy will do with her tooth. Next, have each child write and illustrate on a pillow cutout what he thinks the tooth fairy does with the teeth she collects. *Writing*

Wednesday

Morning Group Time: Lead students in a game of The Tooth Fairy Says by giving two-step directions for them to follow. For example, say, "The Tooth Fairy says, 'Pretend to look under your pillow and then hop up and down.'" Encourage youngsters to follow the directions. *Following two-step directions*

Read-Alouds and Art:

Say Cheese!
(See directions on page 140.)

Thursday

Morning Group Time: Gather plastic food models or food pictures, including some foods that are good for teeth and some that are not. Enlarge and cut out two tooth patterns (see page 141). On one tooth, mask the smiley face, draw a sad face, and attach a piece of aluminum foil (cavity). Invite students to help you sort each food onto the appropriate tooth. *Identifying healthy foods for teeth*

Read-Alouds and Art: Read aloud *Arthur's Tooth* by Marc Brown. After sharing the story, review some of the ways that were recommended for ridding Arthur of his loose tooth. Then have youngsters brainstorm other possibilities for removing baby teeth. List students' ideas on a large tooth cutout. *Creative thinking*

Friday

Morning Group Time: Give each child a length of dental floss or yarn. Direct students to listen as you say words aloud. When they hear a word that begins with /fl/ like *floss,* have them move their floss in the air as if they were flossing. *Blends*

Read-Alouds and Art:

Floss Painting
(See directions on page 140.)

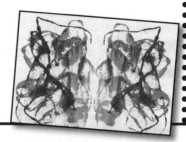

Literacy and Math

Program each of three toothpaste tube cutouts (see page 141) with a different word family. Also program each cutout in a class supply of small tooth cutouts (see page 141) with a corresponding word-family word. (Repeat words if needed.) Give each child a tooth and have him place it onto the appropriate tube.
Word families

Give each child a pillow cutout and several imitation coins. Then announce a desired coin set, such as two pennies and one nickel. Have each child pretend to be the tooth fairy and place the corresponding coin set on her pillow. Repeat with different coin combinations.
Identifying coins

Write a different rime on two mouth-shaped cutouts. Then program a supply of small tooth cutouts (pattern on page 141) with words from each word family and a few words that belong to neither group. A child sorts the tooth cutouts onto the mouth shapes, setting aside any words that are not matches. **Word families**

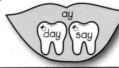

Pair students and give each duo an empty toothpaste box or a clean toothbrush. Have each twosome use its item to measure designated objects in the classroom.
Nonstandard measurement

Survey the group to determine toothpaste flavors students have tried. Make a card for each flavor named and place it in a pocket chart. Have each child write her name on a small tooth cutout (see page 141) and place it in the chart. Then ask questions about the resulting graph. **Graphing**

Song

(sung to the tune of "Shoo Fly")

Brush your teeth up and down,
Back and forth, all around.
Visit your dentist too.
This keeps teeth healthy for you.

Opposites: Guide students to notice the opposite pairs in the song: up, down; back, forth.

Journal Prompts

- Draw your healthy smile. Write about how you keep it that way.

- Draw what you think the tooth fairy looks like. Write about him or her.

- Draw your favorite healthy snack. Write about it.

- Write about a trip to the dentist. Illustrate your writing.

- Write and complete the following sentence: My teeth are important because _____. Illustrate your writing.

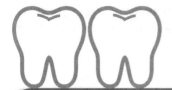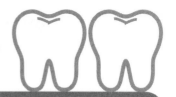
Say Cheese!

Materials for one picture: cutout smile from a close-up photo of the child's mouth, sheet of construction paper, crayons, scrap paper, glue

Steps:
1. Draw your portrait (head, shoulders, and hand for holding a toothbrush) on the paper.
2. Glue the photo of your smile on your portrait.
3. Use the paper scraps to make a toothbrush.
4. Glue the toothbrush to your paper.

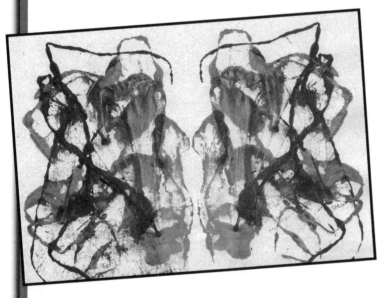

Floss Painting

Materials for one painting: 12" x 18" sheet of construction paper, lengths of dental floss, shallow pans of paint

Steps:
1. Fold the paper in half and then unfold it.
2. Drag a length of dental floss through one color of paint and place it on one half of the paper, leaving the paint-free end of the floss off the paper.
3. Refold the paper and smooth your hand over the surface.
4. Pull out the floss to make a design inside the paper.
5. Repeat the process with several different colors of paint.

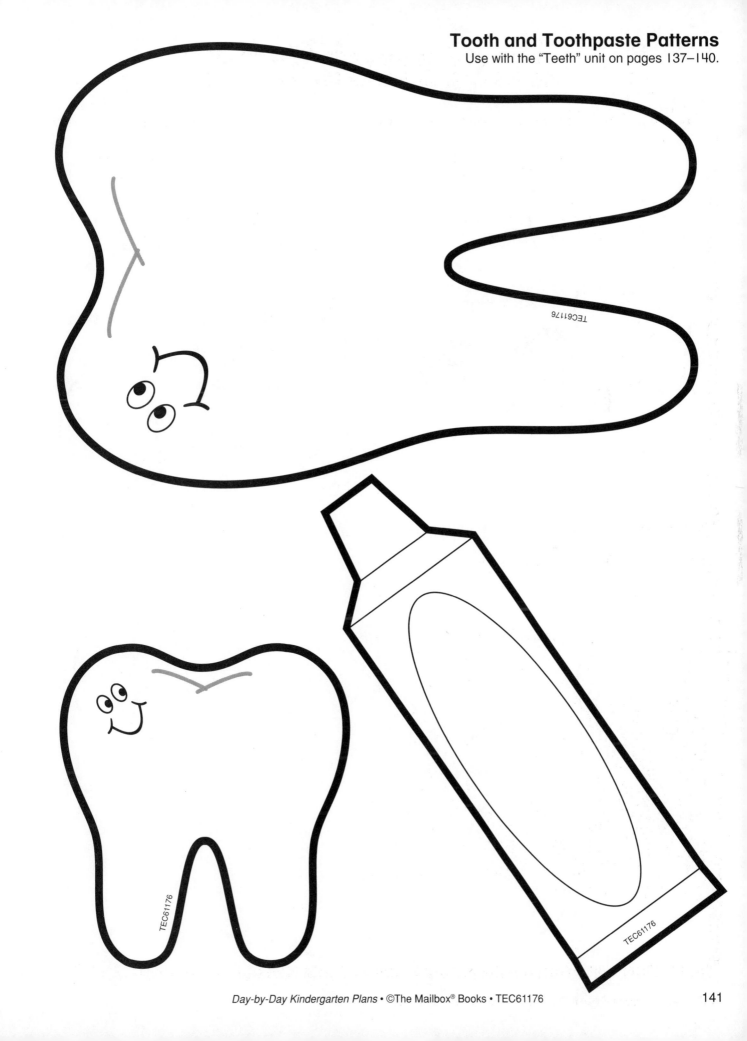

TEC61176

TEC61176

TEC61176

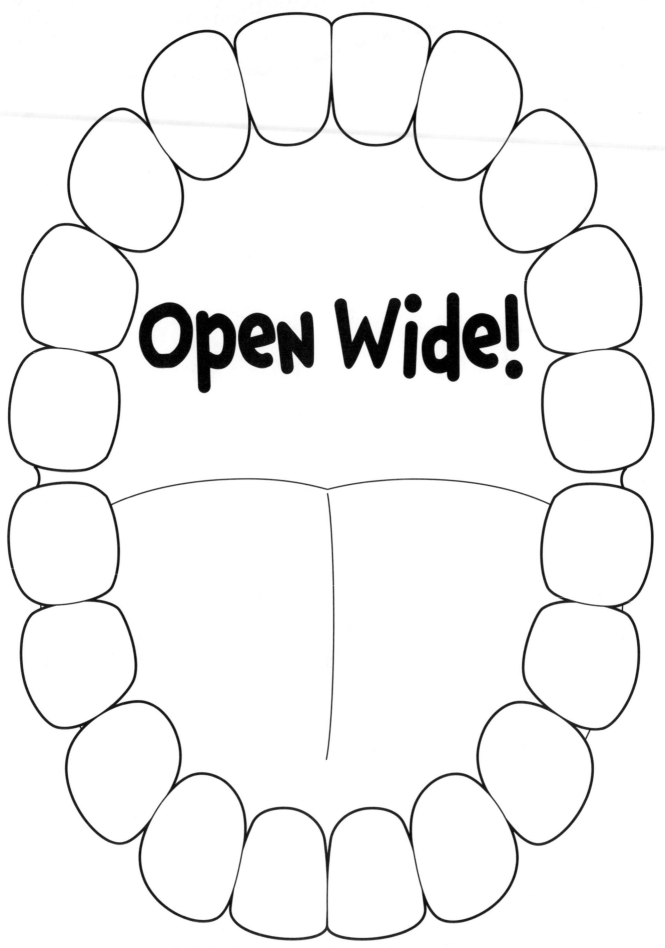

Open Wide!

Day-by-Day Kindergarten Plans • ©The Mailbox® Books • TEC61176

142   **Note to the teacher:** Use with the "Teeth" unit on pages 137–140.

Space
Centers for the Week

ABC Center: Label an enlarged moon cutout (pattern on page 147) with the word *moon* and underline the *n*. Cut out a copy of the picture cards from page 148. A student places the pictures whose names end with /n/ like *moon* on the moon cutout. ***Ending sound /n/***

Reading Center: Place high-frequency word cards facedown in a column. Place a space shuttle cutout at the bottom of the cards and a moon cutout at the top (patterns on page 147). A child turns over the first card above the shuttle and reads the word. Then he removes the card and slides the shuttle closer to the moon. He continues until the rocket reaches the moon. ***High-frequency words***

Math Center: Cut out several copies of the moon pattern from page 147. On some of the cutouts, shade half of the moon; leave the remaining cutouts unshaded. A child sorts them into groups of whole and half moons. ***Fractions***

Art Center: Set out black construction paper, foil star stickers, and white crayons. A student attaches the stars to her paper to create a new constellation. Then she uses the crayon to draw lines connecting the stars. Finally, she names her constellation and writes the name on her paper. ***Artistic expression***

Science Center: Provide cardboard circles, foil, dried pasta, small pom-poms, milk jug lids, play dough, and glue. To make a model of the moon's bumpy surface, a child glues desired items to the circle, attaching the lids with small bits of play dough. After the glue dries, he molds foil over the surface of the collage. ***Making a model***

Morning Group Time	Read-Alouds and Art
Monday — Locate your state on a globe, mark it with a sticker, and have a volunteer shine a flashlight (sun) on it. Explain that when this part of Earth faces the sun, it is daytime. Slowly turn the globe until your state is on the side opposite the flashlight. Explain that as this part of Earth rotates away from the sun, it becomes nighttime. **Understanding day and night**	Read aloud *Me and My Place in Space* by Joan Sweeney. Then revisit the last six pages of the book. Instruct each child to fold a sheet of paper in half and then unfold it. Direct him to draw himself in his world on the left side of the paper. Then have him imagine what another world might be like and draw himself in that world on the right side of the paper. ***Responding to literature***
Tuesday — Give each student a star cutout (pattern on page 147). Announce words, including some beginning with /st/ like *star*. A child holds up his star each time he hears a word beginning with /st/. **Blend /st/**	Read aloud *I Want to Be an Astronaut* by Byron Barton. Then discuss with students why they would or would not like to be astronauts. ***Responding to literature***
Wednesday — Attach Sticky-Tac to the back of a set of number cards from 1 to 10. Ask a volunteer to arrange the numbers on a wall to count down from 10 to 1. Invite another child to point to the numbers as the class squats and counts down from 10. Then have everyone announce, "Blast off!" as they jump up at 1. **Counting backward**	**Amazing Astronauts** *(See directions on page 146.)* 
Thursday — Invite one student to hold a large sun cutout and another to hold a large Earth cutout. Have the earth slowly walk around the sun. Explain that Earth travels around the sun in a circle called an *orbit*. Repeat the activity with Earth and moon cutouts to demonstrate the moon's orbit around Earth. **Understanding orbits**	As you read aloud *When the Moon Smiled* by Petr Horacek, pause after each spread of pages and invite students to count the animals and stars with you. Assign each of ten small groups of students one of the animals from the story. Have all youngsters stand. As you reread the story, direct each group to sit when they hear their animal mentioned. **Listening**
Friday — Describe for students an imaginary astronaut's day. Have a student show the time on a practice clock as you name a specific time for each activity, such as "He eats breakfast at 6:00" or "At 3:00, she goes for a spacewalk." **Time to the hour**	**Super Suns!** *(See directions on page 146.)* 

Literacy and Math

Write the name of each planet on a separate card. Number three columns of a pocket chart. Read aloud each planet name and have students clap the word parts. Then place the card in the chart under the corresponding number of syllables. **Phonological awareness**

Direct each child to fold a sheet of white construction paper in half and then unfold it. Have him draw with crayons something he does in the daytime on the top half of his paper and something he does at night on the bottom half. Then instruct him to paint over the daytime picture with diluted yellow paint and paint over the nighttime picture with diluted black paint.

Post a large yellow circle. Cut a supply of yellow paper strips. Decide on a skill to review, such as beginning or ending sounds. Announce a word. If students correctly name the letter for the beginning (or ending) sound, have a youngster attach a ray to the sun. Continue with different words. **Letter-sound association**

Number star cutouts (pattern on page 147) from 1 to 20. Place the stars in your pocket chart in order, omitting one of the stars. Sing the song below. Then have students determine which star is missing and put it in place. Repeat the activity with different numbers. **Number order**

Twinkle, twinkle, can you see
Which star's missing? Please tell me.

Choose two or three different rimes and use a white crayon to write each one a separate piece of black paper. Program a supply of star cutouts with words that have the rimes. Have students help sort the stars onto the corresponding night sky. **Word families**

Song

(sung to the tune of
"The Wheels on the Bus")

Rockets fly into outer space.
It's a big and lonely place.
Planets spin round. The moon glows
    bright.
The stars make twinkling light.

Rhyming: Ask students to name the two rhyming word pairs. Then challenge youngsters to name other words (real and nonsense) that rhyme with each pair.

Journal Prompts

- Imagine what it would be like to live on the moon. Write about it. Illustrate your writing.

- Pretend you are an astronaut. Write about your trip into space. Illustrate your writing.

- Write and complete the following sentence: "The sun is important because _____." Illustrate your writing.

- There is no sound on the moon. If you lived there, what would you miss hearing the most? Write about it.

- Write about a newly discovered planet. Illustrate your writing.

Instructions

Amazing Astronauts

Materials for one astronaut: small paper plate, skin-tone paper circle the diameter of the center of the plate, foil, plastic wrap, crayons, tape

Steps:

1. Cover the plate with foil and mold the foil to the shape of the plate.
2. Draw your face on the skin-tone circle and tape it to the center of the plate.
3. Wrap a piece of plastic wrap over the plate to look like the front of an astronaut's helmet. Tape it in place on the back of the plate.

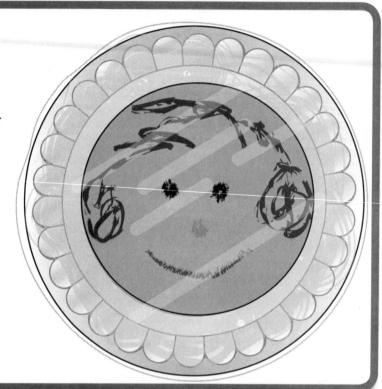

Super Suns!

Materials for one sun: polystyrene foam bowl; sheet of white construction paper; tagboard circle cut to fit inside the bottom of the bowl; orange and yellow paper scraps; orange, yellow, red, and white paint; craft stick; glue

Steps:

1. Squirt a small amount of each color of paint into the bottom of the bowl.
2. Use the craft stick to swirl, but not mix, the colors together.
3. Carefully place the tagboard circle on top of the paint and gently press down until the surface of the circle is covered in paint.
4. Remove the circle and gently press it onto the sheet of paper. Then lift off the circle and discard it.
5. Tear orange and yellow paper scraps and glue them around the sun to form rays.

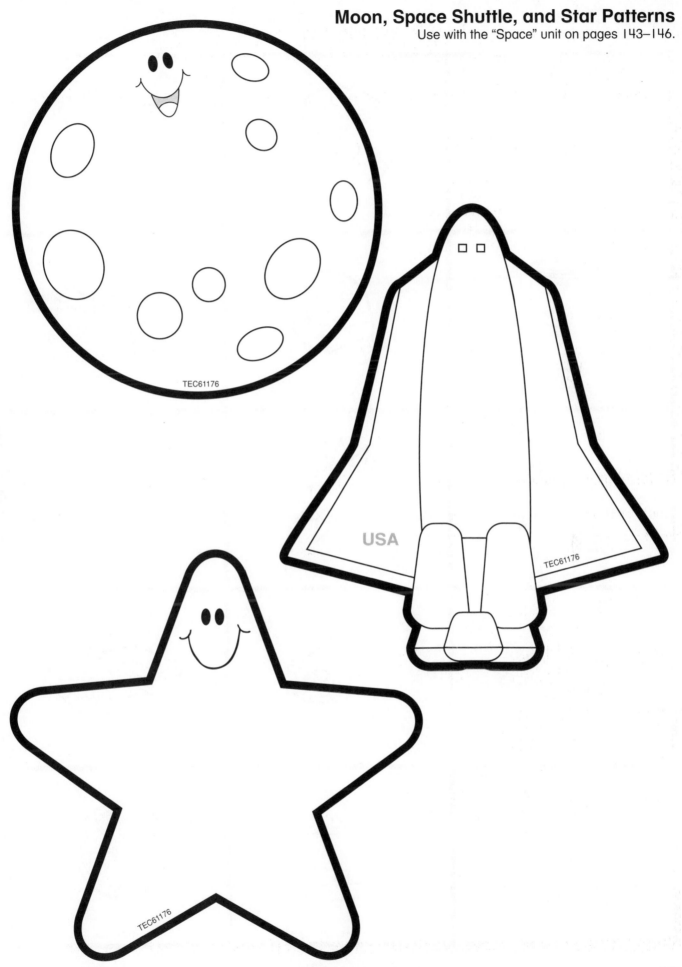

TEC61176

USA

TEC61176

TEC61176

Picture Cards

Use with the "Space" unit on pages 143–146.

TEC61176	TEC61176	TEC61176
TEC61176	TEC61176	TEC61176
TEC61176	TEC61176	TEC61176
TEC61176	TEC61176	TEC61176
TEC61176	TEC61176	TEC61176

Day-by-Day Kindergarten Plans • ©The Mailbox® Books • TEC61176

Dr. Seuss

Centers for the Week

ABC Center: A student chooses a consonant. She draws a self-portrait at the bottom of a vertically positioned sheet of paper. Then she draws balanced on top of her head ten items whose names begin with her letter. On a sentence strip, she writes, "Ten [_B_] things up on top!" *Letter-sound association*

Reading Center: Draw a large red-and-white striped hat on poster board. Divide each stripe in half vertically and write a different high-frequency word in each section. A child stands a distance away and tosses a beanbag on the hat. Then he reads the word on which the beanbag lands. *High-frequency words*

Writing Center: Set out a class supply of large raindrop cutouts. A child thinks about the rainy-day games the Cat in the Hat plays. Then she draws her own favorite rainy-day activity on one side of the raindrop and writes about it on the other side. *Writing*

Math Center: Use the fish card on page 153 to make a supply of red, blue, white, and green fish in a variety of sizes so they resemble the fish from the story *One Fish, Two Fish, Red Fish, Blue Fish.* Place the fish at the center and encourage youngsters to sort them as desired. *Sorting*

Game Center: For this partner game, use the pattern on page 153 to make a large red-and-white striped hat. Arrange a copy of the cards from page 154 facedown at the center. In turn, a child flips over two cards. If the pictures' names rhyme, he places the cards on the hat. If they do not, he turns them back over. Play continues until all the cards are on the hat. *Rhyming*

Morning Group Time	Read-Alouds and Art
Monday Use Dr. Seuss's zany characters to reinforce the differences between make-believe and reality. First, have each child color and cut out an enlarged hat pattern from page 153 and glue it to a paper headband. Then announce statements, some real and some make-believe, inspired by Dr. Seuss books. Have students wear their hats when they hear make-believe statements. *Reality/make-believe* (Make-believe!) (Cats wear hats and talk.)	Cut out a class supply of left (red) and right (blue) child-size foot patterns. Read aloud *The Foot Book*. After reading, tape a red foot and a blue foot in front of each child. Then reread the story and have youngsters step on the appropriate foot whenever they hear "right foot" or "left foot." *Listening, left and right*
Tuesday In *The Cat in the Hat,* the cat visits the children's home while their mom is out. Discuss with students the possible dangers of letting a stranger in the house. Then ask students to imagine how the story might have been different if the Cat in the Hat had not been allowed inside. *Creative thinking*	**Cat in the Hat** *(See directions on page 152.)* 
Wednesday Give each child ten counters and an enlarged copy of the fish card on page 153 that has been programmed with number words from one to ten. Announce a number word and have each child cover the appropriate word with a counter. Continue until all the words are covered. *Number words*	Read aloud *My Many Colored Days*. Set out a supply of colorful paper strips. Have each child choose a few strips and tell how each color makes her feel; then help her write her response on the appropriate strip. Finally, guide her in taping her strips together to make a chain. *Responding to literature*
Thursday Label two columns in a pocket chart with the names of two Dr. Seuss characters. Write on cards words that describe the two characters. Read each word aloud and have students decide which character the word best describes. Place the card under the corresponding character's name. *Comparing characters*	**Tasty Ham and Eggs** *(See directions on page 152.)* 
Friday Enlist students' help in creating a list of familiar Dr. Seuss books. Help each child label a blank card with the title of his favorite Dr. Seuss book. Then have him place his card in a pocket chart to create a graph of students' favorites. *Graphing*	Read aloud *There's a Wocket in My Pocket!* Revisit selected pages and ask students to name the nonsense words. Then write on the board "There's a ____ in the school." Have students make up creatures by naming words that rhyme with *school*. Write each name on a sentence strip. Then reread the sentence, substituting a new creature. *Rhyming words*

Literacy and Math

In *Ten Apples Up on Top!* the animals balance ten apples on top of their heads. Ask each child to think of something he would like to balance. Have him draw a picture of his head with the ten items on top. Next, invite ten students to stand holding their papers as the remaining students count the items by ten. ***Counting by tens***

Dr. Seuss is known for his imaginative characters, especially the Cat in the Hat. Have students create characters that have rhyming names, such as the Pig in the Wig or the Dog in the Fog. List the names of students' creations on the board. ***Rhyming words***

Give each child five red and five blue fish cards (pattern on page 153). Announce a number from one to five and have each child put that many red fish on his work area. Then announce another number from one to five and have him put that many blue fish on his work area. Then lead students in determining the total number of fish. Repeat the activity with different numbers. ***Adding with manipulatives***

Post the question "How do you like green eggs and ham?" in a pocket chart. Write on sentence strips "I like them on a _____" and "I like them with a _____." Select several pairs of rhyming words— such as *beach* and *peach*, *bear* and *chair*, and *rug* and *bug*—and write each word on a different blank card. Lead students in creating and reading pairs of rhyming sentences. ***Making sentences, rhyming***

In *Green Eggs and Ham,* Sam-I-Am names several places where his companion could try green eggs and ham. Invite youngsters to share where they would like to eat a desired food. Have each child cut out a picture of a food from a magazine. After she glues the picture to a paper plate, have her write the name of a fun place where she would like to eat the food. ***Writing***

I would eat pizza in the pool.

Song

(sung to the tune of "She'll Be Comin' Round the Mountain")

Dr. Seuss's books can teach us something new.
They can cheer us up when we are feeling blue.
We will read *Green Eggs and Ham,*
We will laugh at Sam-I-Am,
And we'll *Hop on Pop* and learn ABCs too!

Recalling information: After youngsters sing the song, lead them in recalling information about the stories and character mentioned.

Journal Prompts

- If you could talk to Dr. Seuss, what would you tell him? What would you ask him?

- Draw your favorite Dr. Seuss character. Write about it.

- Write and complete the following sentence: "My favorite thing about Dr. Seuss books is _____." Illustrate your writing.

- If you could be a character in one of Dr. Seuss's books, which character would you be? Write about it. Illustrate your writing.

- Write about your favorite Dr. Seuss book. Tell why you like it. Illustrate your writing.

Instructions

Tasty Ham and Eggs

Materials for one project: green paper scraps, thinned light-green paint, 2 green pom-poms, paper plate, scissors, glue

Steps:
1. Pour a small amount of paint on the plate.
2. Tilt the plate back and forth to make the shape of an egg white.
3. When the paint is dry, glue the green pom-poms (yolks) to the plate.
4. Cut a ham shape from the scrap paper. Glue the ham to the plate.

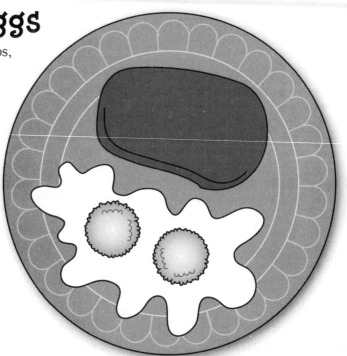

Cat in the Hat

Materials for one cat: 9" x 12" sheet of red tagboard, three 1" x 12" strips of white construction paper, one 3" x 12" black paper strip, 3 thin black paper strips, 2¾" white circle, glue, markers, stapler

Steps:
1. Glue the large black strip to the bottom of the red tagboard.
2. Glue the white strips on the tagboard above the black strip, leaving space between them to form red and white alternating stripes.
3. Draw features on the white circle to make a cat face.
4. Crisscross the three thin black strips and glue them to the face for whiskers.
5. Glue the face in the middle of the black strip.
6. Roll the tagboard into a tube. Have your teacher staple the ends together.

TEC61176

TEC61176

Picture Cards

Use with the "Dr. Seuss" unit on pages 149–152.

TEC61176

TEC61176

TEC61176

TEC61176

TEC61176

TEC61176

TEC61176

TEC61176

TEC61176

TEC61176

TEC61176

TEC61176

Day-by-Day Kindergarten Plans • ©The Mailbox® Books • TEC61176

St. Patrick's Day

Centers for the Week

Game Center: For this partner game, number ten yellow paper circles (gold coins) from 1 to 10. Place the coins in a pot. Two students each take a coin and determine which number is greater. They set that coin aside and return the other coin to the pot. Play continues until only one coin remains. ***Comparing numbers***

Math Center: Set out 25 yellow paper circles (gold coins). A student arranges the coins in groups of five. She then counts by fives to determine the total number. Then, to check her work, she counts each coin individually. ***Counting by fives***

Reading Center: Provide a supply of newspaper pages and green markers. A student chooses a newspaper page and uses a marker to circle each ending punctuation mark. ***Recognizing punctuation***

Art Center: Set out paper, heart-shaped cookie cutters, a paintbrush, and a shallow pan with green paint. A student dips a cookie cutter in paint and makes three prints to resemble the leaves of a shamrock. She repeats the process several times until her paper is filled with shamrocks. ***Fine-motor skills***

Writing Center: Place colored pencils at the center. A student writes colorful sentences on the topic of rainbows. ***Creative writing***

Morning Group Time	Read-Alouds and Art
Monday Program each of several shamrock cutouts (see page 159) with a different high-frequency word. Draw an empty pot on the board and place the shamrocks facedown on the floor. Have a volunteer pick a shamrock and read the word. Then invite her to draw a gold coin in the pot. Select a child to pick another shamrock to continue. **High-frequency words**	Invite students to name things they know about St. Patrick's Day. Record their responses. Read aloud *St. Patrick's Day* by Gail Gibbons. Read the list and draw a shamrock beside those things that were mentioned in the book. Then, with students' help, add new information about the holiday to the list. **Prior knowledge**
Tuesday Program a class supply of yellow paper circles (gold coins) with multiples of five up to 50, repeating numbers as needed. Give each student a coin. Invite the class to count by fives with you. As each child's number is called, have him stand. Collect the coins, redistribute them, and repeat the activity. **Counting by fives**	**Blended-Color Shamrocks** *(See directions on page 158.)*
Wednesday Attach a small shamrock cutout (see page 159) to a craft stick to make a pointer. Write a message of several sentences previewing the day's events. After reading the message, invite students, in turn, to use the pointer to indicate a capital letter or an ending punctuation mark. **Capitalization, ending punctuation**	Show students the cover of *That's What Leprechauns Do* by Eve Bunting. Ask them what types of things they think leprechauns do. After reading the story, invite youngsters to compare their predictions with the story events. **Making predictions**
Thursday Gather a ribbon or bandana in each of the colors of the rainbow and tie them end to end. Have students sit in a circle. As you play a recording of soft music, students feed the bandana "rainbow" around the circle. Stop the music and have students freeze. Hold up a color word card. Invite the child holding the corresponding color to say, "Rainbow [color name]!" **Color words**	Help youngsters find the gold from yesterday's story with this activity. Have students close their eyes as you secretly place a pot-of-gold cutout nearby. Invite students to open their eyes and raise their hands when they see the pot of gold. **Participating in a game**
Friday Say *gold* as you clap once. Then have students clap a classmate's name and say whether the number of syllables in the child's name matches the number of syllables in *gold*. Continue in the same way using the words *shamrock* and *leprechaun*. **Phonological awareness**	**Tissue Paper Rainbow** *(See directions on page 158.)* 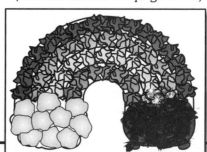

Literacy and Math

Label each of three yellow paper circles (gold coins) with a different ending punctuation mark. Place the coins in a pot. In turn, have a child take a coin and identify the punctuation mark. Then help students generate a telling sentence (period), an asking sentence (question mark), or an excited sentence (exclamation mark), depending on the mark drawn. **Identifying punctuation**

Program pairs of shamrock cutouts (see page 159) with CVC rhyming words. Shuffle the shamrocks and place them facedown on the floor. In turn, have students turn over two cutouts and read the words, providing help as needed. If the words rhyme, set the shamrocks aside. If not, turn them over and continue play. **Rhyming words**

Cut out several copies of the shamrocks on page 159. Use the cutouts to create a pattern in a pocket chart. Have students name the pattern and extend it. Repeat the process several times, creating a new pattern each time. **Patterning**

Tell students to pretend they have a pot of gold. Have them write to describe what they would do with the gold and then draw a picture to match their writing. After each child reads her page to the class, bind the pages behind a cover titled "If We Found the Pot of Gold." Then place the class book in your reading center. **Writing**

I wud by a dog if I fond the gold.

Color ten copies of the leprechaun pattern from page 159 so that each one is wearing different-colored clothing. Cut out the patterns and place them in a row. Ask questions about the order of the leprechauns, such as "Which leprechaun is third?" and "Which place in line is the leprechaun who is wearing purple stripes?" **Ordinal numbers**

Song

St. Patrick's Day
(sung to the tune of "The Muffin Man")

Oh, did you see the leprechaun?
First, he was here, and now he's gone!
He'll snatch that pot of gold away
For it's St. Patrick's Day.

Punctuation: Display the song on chart paper. After students are familiar with the song, have volunteers point to the period, question mark, and exclamation mark.

Journal Prompts

- Draw yourself celebrating St. Patrick's Day. Write about it.

- Draw your favorite green thing. Write about it.

- Imagine you found a lucky shamrock. Write about what happened. Illustrate your writing.

- Draw a leprechaun. Write about him.

- Draw a rainbow. Write and complete the following sentence: "A rainbow is special because _____."

Blended-Color Shamrocks

Materials for one shamrock: white construction paper, shamrock template, yellow-tinted water, blue-tinted water, eyedropper, scissors

Steps:
1. Trace the shamrock onto the paper and cut out the tracing.
2. Using the eyedropper, put a few drops of the blue-tinted water onto the shamrock. Place drops of the yellow-tinted water on top of the blue drops to create a green splotchy design.
3. Set the cutout aside to dry.

Tissue Paper Rainbow

Materials for one rainbow: copy of page 160, small tissue paper squares in four different rainbow colors, glue, cotton balls, gold glitter, crayons

Steps:
1. Choose a color of tissue paper. Crumple one of the squares and dip it in glue. Then press the tissue paper onto the rainbow. Continue with that color until the arc is completed.
2. Repeat Step 1 with each of the remaining three colors of tissue paper.
3. Glue cotton balls onto the cloud.
4. Color the pot. Then apply glue to the top of the pot and sprinkle glitter over the glue.

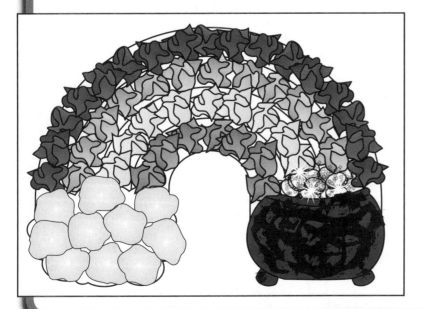

TEC61176

TEC61176

TEC61176

TEC61176

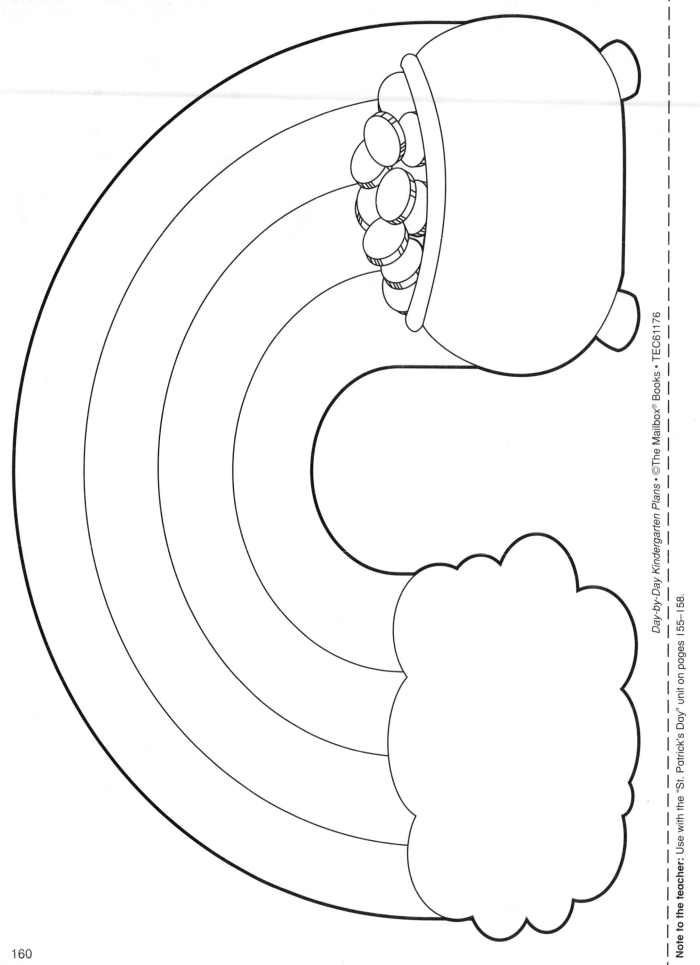

160

Note to the teacher: Use with the "St. Patrick's Day" unit on pages 155–158.

Healthy Eating

Centers for the Week

Writing Center: Cut pictures of foods from a grocery store flyer and attach them to a sheet of poster board. Then label each food. A student chooses items from the poster and writes the words on a paper strip to make a grocery list. *Making a list*

Math Center: Fill your sensory table or tub with dried pasta. Provide bowls of different sizes and a measuring cup. A student estimates how many cups of pasta will fill one of the bowls and then measures to find out. She repeats the process with the other bowls. *Capacity, estimation*

ABC Center: Place in a bag an assortment of plastic food or pictures of food. A student pulls an item from the bag, draws it on his paper, and writes the letter for the beginning sound of the food's name. He places the item aside and repeats the activity until the bag is empty. *Letter-sound association*

Art Center: In advance, slice several fruits and vegetables and place each one beside a different shallow pan of paint. A student presses a fruit or vegetable into the paint and makes prints on a sheet of paper. The child repeats the process with the remaining foods. *Painting*

Fine-Motor Center: Set out a rolling pin, round and square cookie cutters, plastic knives, and play dough. A child rolls the play dough and then uses the cookie cutters to make healthy round foods, such as pancakes and tomato slices, and square snacks, such as bread and cheese slices. Then he divides each food into equal parts. *Equal parts*

Morning Group Time	Read-Alouds and Art
Monday Stock a grocery bag with healthy food items or pictures, making sure there is an item that starts with the same beginning sound as each child's name in the class. Remove an item from the bag and have students name it. Invite each child whose name begins with the same sound to stand. Greet these students and continue with another item from the bag. ***Beginning sounds***	Read aloud *Bread and Jam for Frances* by Russell Hoban. Then discuss with students why it's important to eat a variety of foods. ***Promoting healthy eating***
Tuesday Cut pictures of healthy and unhealthy foods from grocery store flyers. Then glue the pictures to separate cards and place them in a grocery bag. Invite a child to select a card and determine whether the food is healthy. If it is, he puts the card in a lunchbox. If it isn't, he puts the card in a discard pile. ***Sorting and classifying by one attribute*** 	Invite students to tell about their favorite lunch foods. Read aloud *Lunch* by Denise Fleming. Write "fruits" and "vegetables" on the board. Review the book page by page and, with student input, make a tally mark under the appropriate word for each fruit or vegetable the mouse ate. ***Tallying***
Wednesday Write a morning message previewing the day's events and include one or two healthy eating tips. After reading and discussing the message, have students help count the sentences in it. Record the number of sentences at the end of the message. ***Concepts of print***	Revisit yesterday's story. Then have each child make a mini mouse booklet (see directions on page 164). ***Identifying fruits and vegetables*** 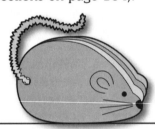
Thursday Make a sign for each of the five main food groups. Divide the class into five groups and give each group a sign. Name a food item and have youngsters in the corresponding group stand. Repeat as time allows. ***Identifying foods in a food group***	Read *Healthy Snacks* by Mari C. Schuh. After sharing the book, encourage students to name healthy snacks as you record their suggestions on the board. Ask each youngster to choose his favorite snack from the list. ***Speaking to express an opinion***
Friday Prepare fruit salad with three different fruits. Have each child place a scoop of salad on a paper plate. Instruct her to use the fruit pieces to make a pattern on the plate. Have her read the pattern and then eat the fruit. ***Patterning***	**Healthy Sandwich** *(See directions on page 164.)* 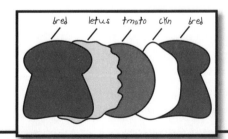

Literacy and Math

Cut out an enlarged copy of the food cards from page 165. Place them in a pocket chart with a price tag of ten cents or less beside each one. Give each child in a small group ten imitation pennies. Each student selects one or more items from the board and "buys" them by counting out her pennies. **Counting pennies**

Have each child write and illustrate on a sheet of paper a sentence about her favorite healthy food. Compile students' pages into a class book titled "Our Healthy Food Book." Invite each child to read her page to the class. **Writing**

Discuss the five main food groups with students. On a blank card, have each child draw and label his favorite food group. Then help youngsters place their cards in a pocket chart to make a graph. **Graphing**

Instruct each child to plan a balanced meal by cutting out magazine pictures of foods. Then have her glue the pictures on a paper plate and use a marker to label each of the foods. **Writing labels**

Use food—such as bananas, apples, or graham crackers—to demonstrate equal and unequal parts. For example, show students a peeled banana and then have a youngster cut it into two equal parts. Repeat the process, having a child cut a banana into unequal parts. **Equal and unequal parts**

Song

Good for You
(sung to the tune of "Are You Sleeping?")

Eat your veggies
And your fruits too.
They are so
Good for you.
Carrots, beans, and green peas,
Eat them up, won't you please?
Apples too.
Good for you!

Beginning and ending sounds:
Display the song on chart paper. After students are familiar with the song, have volunteers locate and point to the beginning and ending sounds of various words.

Journal Prompts

- Draw something healthy you ate yesterday. Write about it.

- Draw food from each of the five main food groups. Label your picture.

- Draw a healthy hot or cold breakfast.

- Draw a healthy lunch you would like to fix for a friend. Write about it.

- Would you rather have a carrot or an orange for a snack? Draw a picture and write about which one you would choose and why.

Instructions

Mini Mouse Booklet

Getting ready: Cut a class supply of teardrop-shaped pages from gray, white, orange, yellow, green, blue, purple, red, and pink construction paper (one page of each per student). Provide markers, crayons, and pipe cleaners for students to use. Have *Lunch* by Denise Fleming available for student reference.

Steps for one booklet:
1. Using a marker, add mouse ear and face details to the gray page to make the cover.
2. Draw the food the mouse ate in the story on each appropriately colored page.
3. Stack the pages behind the cover and punch a hole for the tail.
4. Bind the pages together with a pipe cleaner tail.

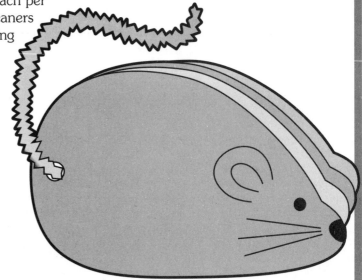

Healthy Sandwich

Materials for one project: sheet of 9" x 12" construction paper, 2 bread slice cutouts, construction paper scraps, scissors, glue, crayons

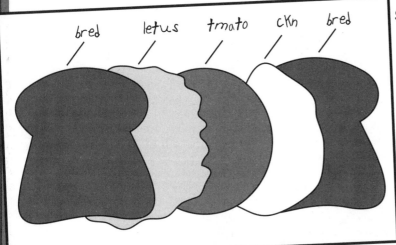

Steps:
1. Cut desired sandwich fillings from the paper scraps.
2. Arrange the bread slices and sandwich fillings on the sheet of construction paper, as shown, and glue them in place.
3. Label the bread and fillings.

TEC61176

TEC61176

TEC61176

TEC61176

TEC61176

TEC61176

TEC61176

TEC61176

TEC61176

TEC61176

TEC61176

TEC61176

TEC61176

TEC61176

TEC61176

Grocery Shopping

✂ Cut. 🖊 Glue on the correct bag.

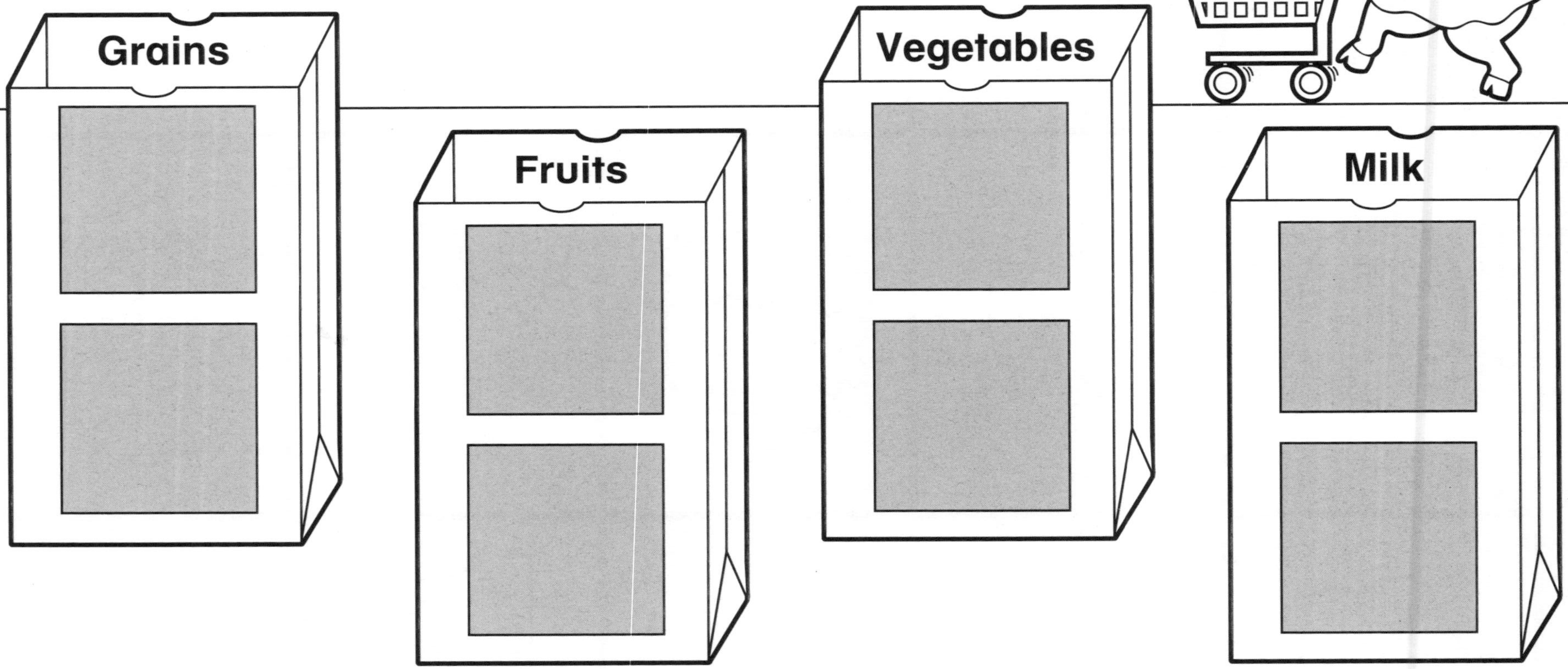

Milk

Vegetables

Fruits

Grains

Day-by-Day Kindergarten Plans • ©The Mailbox® Books • TEC61176

YOGURT
6 OZ.

MILK MILK

Weather

Centers for the Week

Reading Center: Provide a copy of the weather cards on page 171 and a set of matching word cards. Also provide a toy microphone, weather-related books, and a pointer. In a pocket chart, place a sentence strip reading "It is _____ today." A student chooses a word card and picture card to complete the sentence. Then she uses the props to deliver the weather forecast. ***Reading***

Math Center: Label each of four gray cloud shapes with a different coin cutout. Label white snowflake cutouts with corresponding coin values. A student places the snowflakes below the appropriate clouds. ***Identifying coins and their values***

Game Center: For this partner game, a student rolls a die and places a matching number of cotton balls (clouds) on a sheet of blue paper (sky). She writes that number on a whiteboard. Next, her partner repeats the process and they work together to add the numbers. Then they count the clouds to check their work. ***Adding using concrete objects***

ABC Center: Label separate puddle cutouts with different letters of the alphabet. Place the cutouts in a basket on the floor. A youngster removes the cutouts from the basket and places them in a row on the floor in alphabetical order. ***Alphabetical order***

Science Center: Use wooden blocks to create a simple maze. Provide a feather, cotton ball, wad of tissue paper, and small ball. A child blows gently through a straw to guide one of the objects through the maze. He repeats the activity with the other items and observes how much wind is needed to move each one. ***Observing wind power***

Morning Group Time	Read-Alouds and Art
Monday Write the name of each weather type (rainy, snowy, cloudy, sunny, windy, foggy) on a different sheet of chart paper. Invite students to describe each form of weather using descriptive language. Add art around each word as desired. ***Using descriptive words*** 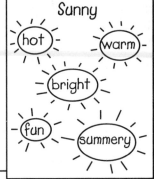	Invite students to name weather words as you write them on a board. Have them listen for those words as you read aloud *What Will the Weather Be Like Today?* by Paul Rogers. After reading, review the list and note which words were in the story. ***Prior knowledge***
Tuesday Write a morning message that previews the day's events and tells the day's weather forecast. Provide weather-related pointers. After reading the message, invite a volunteer to use the pointer that best matches the day's weather to identify the weather words in the message. ***Identifying weather words***	Revisit the page in yesterday's book that shows the frog in the bog. Point out that the words *frog* and *bog* rhyme. Reread the story and invite each student to raise her hand when she hears other pairs of rhyming words. Have a child name the word pair. Write the words on your board. ***Rhyming***
Wednesday Have students name different types of weather as you write the weather words on your board. Next, have students identify the season usually associated with each type of weather as well as other characteristics of that season. ***Speaking***	**Rainy-Day Art** *(See directions on page 170.)* 
Thursday Write the names of different types of weather across the bottom of your board. Have each child write her name on a card and affix it above her favorite type of weather. Discuss the resulting graph. ***Graphing***	Place in a bag a set of weather cards (see page 171). Read *Hello, Sun!* by Dayle Ann Dodds. Have a volunteer pull a card from the bag and name an item of clothing he would wear in that weather. Return the card to the bag and repeat. ***Identifying weather-related clothing***
Friday Fill separate containers with warm, room temperature, and cold water. Place a thermometer in each container and a sheet of paper in front of each one. Have each student place a red dot sticker in front of the container he believes has the warm water, a yellow dot in front of the room temperature water, and a blue dot in front of the cold water. Discuss how to read a thermometer and then reveal the answers to the group. ***Describing temperature***	**World of Weather** *(See directions on page 170.)*

Literacy and Math

For each child, accordion-fold a strip of paper four times and make a weather booklet similar to the one shown. Direct youngsters to write the weather word and draw a matching picture for each day. ***Writing, observing weather***

Prepare for each child a workmat displaying two clouds. Tell youngsters how many blue pom-poms (raindrops) to put on each cloud. Help students count the raindrops in each set. Then have them count the raindrops altogether. ***Adding by combining sets***

Label a copy of the weather cards on page 171 with the name of each weather type. Cut the cards apart and attach each one to a separate resealable bag. In each bag, place letter cards that spell the weather word. Distribute the bags and have students work in pairs to arrange the cards to spell the weather word. ***Matching letters***

For each child, squirt white paint on one half of a sheet of blue construction paper. Instruct youngsters to fold their papers, pressing the paint between the halves. Then have them open their papers and observe the clouds they made. On a separate sheet of paper, have each child write to describe his cloud. ***Writing***

Display a pattern using weather-themed cutouts. Invite a volunteer to add more shapes to extend the pattern. Repeat the process with several other patterns. Next, encourage students to create patterns and call on classmates to extend them. ***Patterning***

Song

(sung to the tune of "He's Got the Whole World in His Hands")

The weather can be different every day.
There might be rain or sun so you can play.
Sometimes the wind blows leaves all around.
In winter, snow falls to the ground.

Syllables: After singing the song several times, call out words from the song and ask students to clap the syllables in the words.

Journal Prompts

- Draw your favorite kind of weather. Write about it.

- Draw yourself in the summer. Write and complete the following sentence: "I wear _____ when it is hot."

- Draw something you like to do when it is hot. Write about it.

- Draw yourself in the winter. Write and complete the following sentence: "I wear _____ when it is cold."

- Draw something you like to do when it is cold. Write about it.

 # Instructions

Rainy-Day Art

Materials for one picture: blue-tinted corn syrup, wallpaper scraps, sheet of white or light-blue construction paper, craft stick, crayons, scissors

Steps:

1. Draw a picture of yourself.
2. Cut a raincoat, boots, and an umbrella from wallpaper scraps. Attach them to your self-portrait.
3. Dip the craft stick in the blue syrup. Drip syrup on the paper to make small raindrops.
4. Let the picture dry on a flat surface for several days.

World of Weather

Materials for one project: light-blue circle cutout divided into fourths, craft materials, crayons, markers

Steps:

1. Designate each section of the circle with a different type of weather. Then in each section, draw a portrait of yourself wearing clothing appropriate for the weather type.
2. Use various craft items to embellish each picture.

TEC61176

TEC61176

TEC61176

TEC61176

TEC61176

TEC61176

What Do I Need?

 Cut.

Glue each item by the weather in which it would be used.

Spring

Centers for the Week

Writing Center: Place a length of green bulletin board paper on a table. A child draws and cuts from magazines spring-related plants and animals and glues them to the paper. Then he uses a marker to label his items. After each child has visited the center, display the resulting spring-related mural. *Labeling pictures*

Science Center: Stock a center with dried grass, newspaper, twigs, twine, yarn, ribbon, and cotton batting. A student uses the materials to build a model of a bird's nest in a disposable bowl. On a sheet of paper, he draws and writes the name of the bird (real or pretend) that he imagines will live in the nest. *Investigating living things*

Math Center: Cut out several copies of the chick and egg patterns on page 177. Program each chick to show a different time to the hour and write each corresponding digital time on an egg half. A student pairs each chick with its matching egg. *Time to the hour*

Reading Center: For this partner game, each student writes a high-frequency word on a blank card with a white crayon. To reveal the words, the partners exchange cards, and each student makes it "rain" by painting over her card with diluted blue paint. Then they identify their words. *High-frequency words*

Art Center: Set out several ink pads in bright colors. A student draws a springtime picture on a sheet of paper. He adds fingerprints to his picture and then uses a marker to add details so each print resembles a bunny. *Artistic expression*

Morning Group Time	Read-Alouds and Art
Monday Write a springtime morning message, making sure it contains both statements and questions, but omitting the ending punctuation marks. After reading, help students determine whether a period or a question mark is needed to complete each sentence. Then invite volunteers to add the correct marks. ***Using ending punctuation***	Draw a large raindrop on chart paper. Invite youngsters to tell what they know about spring as you list their responses on the chart. Read aloud *Flowers and Showers: A Spring Counting Book* by Rebecca Fjelland Davis. ***Prior knowledge***
Tuesday Invite ten students (frogs) to sit in a row in front of the class. Then give each frog a numeral card corresponding to his place in the row. Call out an ordinal number and encourage the frog in that place to hop in the air and then sit down again. Continue in the same way with the remaining frogs. ***Ordinal numbers***	Review yesterday's list. Then reread yesterday's story selection. Enlist students' help in using information from the book to add to the spring list. Then invite youngsters to share what they enjoy about spring.
Wednesday Give each child a simple kite cutout programmed with a number word from one to ten. Call out a number and have each student holding a kite with the corresponding number word stand and "fly" her kite around the room. Repeat the process with each remaining number. ***Number words***	**Robin Red-Breast** *(See directions on page 176.)* 
Thursday Program each of three sheets of green construction paper with a different rime. Label construction paper strips (earthworms) with corresponding word family words. Invite students to match the worms to the appropriate rimes. ***Word families*** 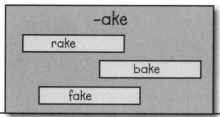	Read aloud *The Earth and I* by Frank Asch. Assign motions for words, phrases, and sentences in the book, such as "The Earth and I are friends," "long walks," and "dance." Invite students to perform the motions during a rereading of the book. ***Participating in an interactive read-aloud***
Friday Write a morning message focusing on Earth Day. On the board, write the words *reduce, reuse,* and *recycle.* Discuss each word's meaning. Under each word, list students' ideas for ways to reduce, reuse, and recycle items in our daily lives. ***Understanding Earth Day***	**Paint the Earth** *(See directions on page 176.)* 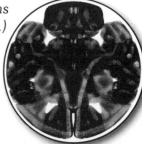

Literacy and Math

Divide the class into small groups and give each group several lengths of brown yarn (earthworms). Instruct each group to work together to order their earthworms from shortest to longest. **Measurement**

Program a construction paper kite with a rime. Tape on a length of yarn for a tail. On each of several bow cutouts, write a word with the same rime, writing the onset on the left half of the bow and the rime on the right half. Then cut the bows apart down the middle. Have students assemble the bows on the kite string and read the resulting words. **Onsets and rimes**

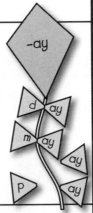

Program a class supply of the clock cards on page 177, each with a different time, repeating times as needed. Label an index card with each clock card's matching digital time. Place the digital time cards in random order in a pocket chart. Then give each child a clock card. Point to a digital time card and have the class announce the time. Then have the student(s) with the matching analog time place his card atop the digital time card. **Telling time**

Program ten large umbrella cutouts with different number words and set out a supply of raindrop cutouts. Point to an umbrella. Have a volunteer read the word on it and place the corresponding number of raindrop cutouts over it. Repeat the process with the remaining umbrellas. **Number words**

Invite two students, in turn, to pretend to be grasshoppers and hop a desired number of times. Ask the seated students to count as each grasshopper hops. On the board, record the number of hops each grasshopper makes. Then announce either "greater" or "less." Invite a volunteer to circle the corresponding number. **Counting, comparing numbers**

Song

(sung to the tune of "Clementine")

In the springtime,
Flowers bloom and
The green grass begins to grow.
We plant new seeds in the garden,
And they soon sprout row by row.

Blends: Guide students to notice that the words *green, grass,* and *grow* have the same beginning sound, just as *springtime* and *sprout* do.

Journal Prompts

- Draw your favorite flower. Write about it.

- Draw your favorite sign of spring. Write about it.

- Draw a butterfly. Write and complete the following sentence: "If I were a butterfly, I would _____."

- Draw the earth. Write three ways you can help keep Earth clean.

- Draw a picture of yourself playing in the rain. Write and complete the following sentence: "When it rains, I like to _____."

Robin Red-Breast

Materials for one robin: brown construction paper rectangle, small red construction paper rectangle, yellow paper scraps, scissors, glue, black marker

Steps:
1. Cut a large oval from the brown paper.
2. Cut a smaller oval from the red paper.
3. Cut a small square from the yellow paper scraps and fold it in half diagonally to form the beak.
4. Glue the pieces together as shown.
5. Use the black marker to add eyes to the project.

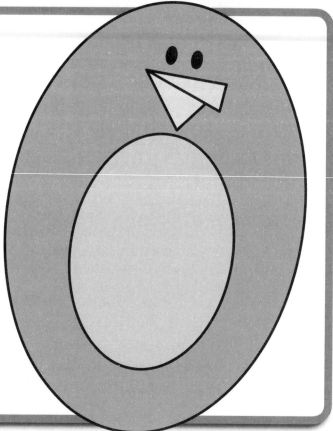

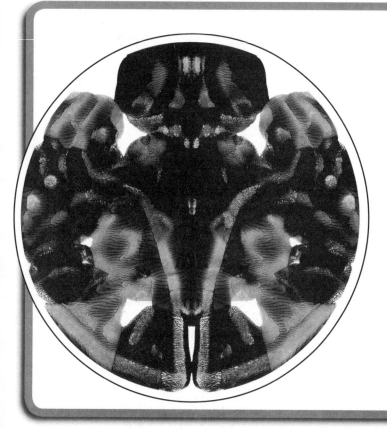

Paint the Earth

Materials for one project: white construction paper circle, green and blue paint

Steps:
1. Fold the circle in half; then unfold it.
2. Place dollops of blue and green paint on one side of the circle.
3. Fold the circle over the paint and rub the outside.
4. Open the circle to reveal a painting that resembles the earth.

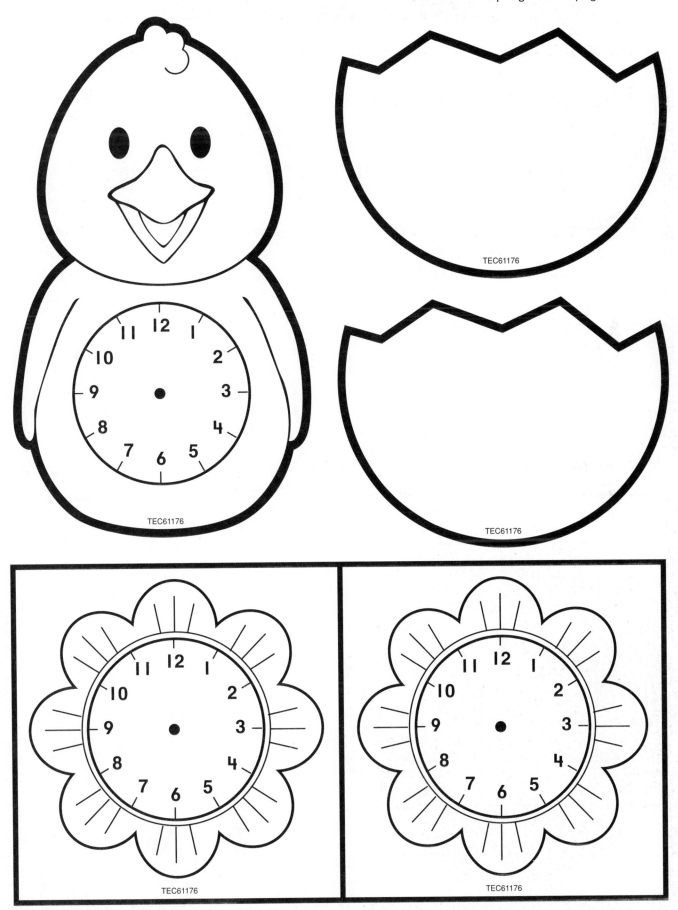

TEC61176

TEC61176

TEC61176

TEC61176

TEC61176

Name_____

Springtime Showers

 Write each time.

         ____

____ : ____   ____ : ____   ____ : ____   ____ : ____

         ____

____ : ____   ____ : ____   ____ : ____   ____ : ____

____ : ____   ____ : ____

Rainy Days

Centers for the Week

Reading Center: Write on each of three puddle cutouts a different familiar rime. Write corresponding word family words on individual raindrop cutouts (patterns on page 183). A student reads the words on the raindrops and puts each one on its matching puddle. ***Word families***

Writing Center: Play a desired audio recording of rain falling. A youngster writes and draws to tell about what he hears. To extend the activity, provide a recording of two types of rainfall, such as a light drizzle and a thunderstorm, for youngsters to compare. ***Writing to describe***

Math Center: Write on each of ten raindrop cutouts (patterns on page 183) a different ordinal number from 1st through 10th. Place the prepared raindrops on a cloud cutout. A child holds the raindrops in her hand and lets them fall on her work area. Then she arranges the raindrops in order under the cloud. ***Ordinal numbers***

Game Center: Write several numbers on a large tagboard puddle cutout. Make a raindrop by filling a blue sock with cotton batting and tying the end. A child tosses the raindrop on the puddle and copies on a sheet of paper the number on which the raindrop lands. His partner takes a turn in a similar manner. Then the twosome compares the numbers and circles the larger one. ***Comparing numbers***

Science Center: Set out a cup of water, eyedroppers, and various materials such as construction paper, a sponge, waxed paper, a plastic plate, cardboard, and a paper towel. A student squeezes a drop of water on each material and makes observations to compare what happens to the water. ***Making observations***

Morning Group Time	Read-Alouds and Art

Monday

Write on chart paper a morning message that includes the word *rain* several times. During a rereading of the message, invite volunteers to circle the word *rain* each time it appears. Then lead students in counting the total number of times the word is circled. Write the number in a raindrop shape beside the message. **Word recognition**

Simulate the sounds of light rain and heavy rain by alternately spraying and streaming water on a metal pan. Then discuss the sounds associated with rain and read aloud *Listen to the Rain* by Bill Martin Jr. and John Archambault. **Prior knowledge**

Tuesday

Give each child a raindrop cutout (see page 183) programmed with a number. Lead youngsters in singing the song below. When a child hears his number, he stands and pretends to be rain falling. When he hears "Thank you," he sits down. **Number recognition**

sung to the tune of "Skip to My Lou"

Raindrops with the number [25],   Rain, rain, falling down,
Raindrops with the number [25],   Rain, rain, falling down,
Raindrops with the number [25],   Rain, rain, falling down,
We're ready for the rainfall!   Thank you for the rainfall!

Revisit yesterday's story to review the different sounds associated with rainfall. Then have each child make a rain stick (see directions on page 182) to simulate rainy day sounds. **Auditory discrimination**

Wednesday

Post a supply of raindrop cutouts. Have youngsters say the word *rain,* emphasizing the initial /r/. Then invite volunteers, in turn, to name other words that begin with /r/. For each word named correctly, remove a raindrop. Continue until the rainy day scene is cleared away! **Beginning sound /r/**

Review with students each of the five senses. Invite youngsters to predict how animals might use their senses to describe rain. Then read aloud *Rain* by Manya Stojic. **Making predictions**

Thursday

Invite students to act like water as you lead them through the water cycle! Post cutouts of a cloud, a sun, and a puddle. Instruct youngsters to sit by the puddle and pretend to be heated by the sun. Next, have students "evaporate" and then slowly "condense" near the cloud shape. Then, after the cloud cools, have little ones "precipitate" back to the puddle. **Water cycle**

Gluey, Gooey Raindrops
(See directions on page 182.)

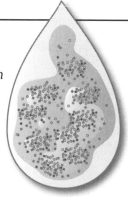

Friday

Display a large closed umbrella. Ask youngsters to name things in the room that they think are *shorter than* or *longer than* the umbrella. Record their responses in a two-column chart. Then lead youngsters in comparing the umbrella with the length of the items they named. Make adjustments to the chart as needed. **Comparing length**

Shorter Than the Umbrella	Longer Than the Umbrella
stapler pencil sharpener	teacher's desk

Show youngsters the front cover of *In the Rain With Baby Duck* by Amy Hest and have them tell how they think Baby Duck feels in the rain. Then have students listen during a read-aloud of the book to find out how Baby Duck's feelings changed from the beginning to the end of the story. **Beginning, middle, and end**

Literacy and Math

Place five different-size puddle shapes on the floor. Have students count and record the number of heel-to-toe steps it takes to measure each puddle. Lead youngsters to use their answers to compare the sizes of the puddles. **Nonstandard measurement**

Ask each child to share what she likes to do on a rainy day. Write each child's name and response on a paper strip. Have her cut between the words and then glue her name and sentence to a sheet of paper. After each child illustrates her work, bind the completed pages. **Word recognition, sentence order**

Have each youngster gently pull cotton balls to make five clouds. Instruct him to glue the clouds across the top of a sheet of paper. Beneath each cloud, help him squeeze blue-tinted glue to make five raindrops. Then lead youngsters in counting by fives to 25. **Counting by fives**

Display two cloud cutouts numbered 1 and 2. Program each of several raindrop cutouts (patterns on page 183) with a one- or two-syllable word, such as *rain, storm, thunder, drizzle,* or *puddle*. In turn, read aloud each word and have youngsters clap to determine how many syllables are in the word. Post each raindrop under the corresponding cloud. **Syllables**

Write a different high-frequency word on each of several puddle cutouts. Invite each youngster, in turn, to toss a raindrop (blue pom-pom) on a puddle and read the word. If she is correct, leave the raindrop on the puddle. If she is incorrect, remove the raindrop. **High-frequency words**

Song

(sung to the tune of "Do Your Ears Hang Low?")

On a rainy day,
It is fun to stay inside.
We can make a tent
And then crawl in it and hide.
Rainy days fill rivers,
And they wash away the snow.
They help gardens grow.

Cause and Effect: Guide students to identify cause-and-effect relationships associated with rainfall.

Journal Prompts

- Draw yourself playing in the rain. Write about it.

- Draw rain gear that you might wear on a rainy day. Write about the items.

- Draw an umbrella. Write and complete the following sentence: "My umbrella is _____."

- Draw an animal playing in the rain. Write about it.

- Draw yourself riding on a rain cloud. Write and complete the following sentence: "When I rode on a rain cloud, I _____."

Instructions

Rhythmic Rain Stick

Materials for one rain stick: cardboard tube, scoop of beans, construction paper strip, two construction paper circles, crayons, tape, glue

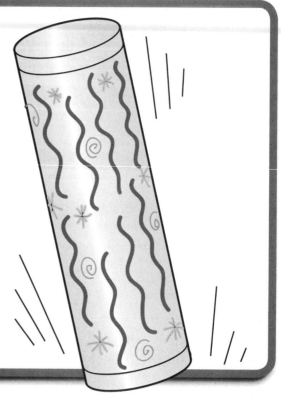

Steps:
1. Draw designs on the construction paper strip. Keeping the designs on the outside, glue the strip around the tube.
2. Fold down the edges of a circle around one end of the tube; tape it in place to seal the end.
3. Ask an adult to empty a scoop of beans in your tube.
4. Seal the open end of the tube as in Step 2.

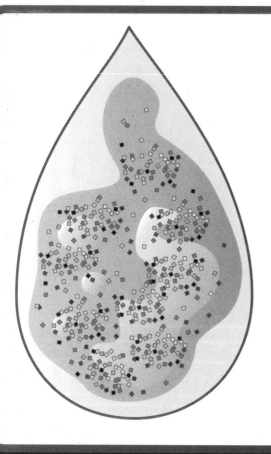

Gluey, Gooey Raindrops

Materials for one raindrop: copy of a raindrop pattern from page 183, two 5" x 6" pieces of Con-tact paper, blue-tinted glue, glitter

Steps:
1. Place one piece of Con-tact paper, sticky-side up, atop the raindrop.
2. Squeeze glue in the middle of the Con-tact paper and sprinkle it with glitter. Using the raindrop pattern to guide you, spread the mixture with your fingers to make a raindrop shape.
3. Lay the second piece of Con-tact paper, sticky-side down, evenly atop the first piece.
4. Press the edges to make a one-inch seal around the raindrop.
5. Carefully trim the sealed paper to complete the raindrop.

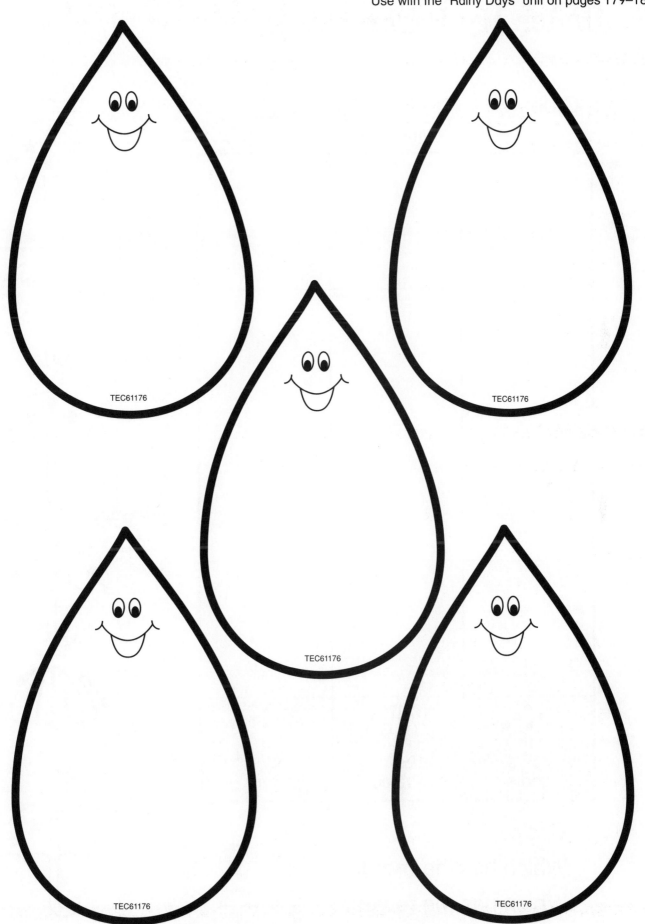

TEC61176

TEC61176

TEC61176

TEC61176

TEC61176

Name _____

Under My Umbrella

 Cut.

Glue.

Umbrellas

spots	stripes	stars

Circle.

Which has the **most?**

Which has the **fewest?**

Day-by-Day Kindergarten Plans • ©The Mailbox® Books • TEC61176

The Farm

Centers for the Week

ABC Center: Write each of several letters on individual potato cutouts. A student "plants" the potatoes in alphabetical order on a length of brown construction paper (soil). *Alphabetical order*

Writing Center: Place toy tractors in a large container of soil. Post a list of high-frequency words at the center. A child moves a tractor through the soil to write each word on the list. *High-frequency words*

Fine-Motor Center: Place at the center copies of the cow from page 189, black construction paper scraps, scissors, and glue. A child cuts out a copy of the cow. Then he tears black paper to make spots and glues them to his cow. *Cutting and tearing*

Math Center: Set out number cards, a supply of yellow pom-poms (chicks), paper, and a pencil. A youngster takes two cards and places the appropriate number of chicks by each card. Then she uses the numbers to write an addition sentence and counts the chicks to check her work. She continues as time permits. *Addition*

Game Center: Each player, in turn, rolls a die and places the corresponding number of play-dough spots on a laminated copy of the cow mat from page 189. Students compare the number of spots on each cow, and the player(s) with the most spots says, "Moo!" Then players remove the spots to start again. *Comparing numbers*

Morning Group Time	Read-Alouds and Art
Monday	

Monday

Have students name adult farm animals and the corresponding baby animals. Record each response on a different card. Then give each card to a student. Have each child make the sound of his animal. Then encourage the youngsters to pair each adult animal with the appropriate baby. *Vocabulary*

Read aloud *Big Red Barn* by Margaret Wise Brown. Post a barn cutout to use as a KWL chart. Record student responses about what they know and what they want to know about farms. Update the chart, including what students learn, throughout the week. *KWL chart*

Tuesday

Post a length of bulletin board paper. Discuss with students animals that live and plants that grow on a farm. Then instruct each youngster to draw farm animals or plants, cut out their drawings, and then glue them to the paper to make a farm scene. *Investigating living things*

Revisit yesterday's story and have youngsters list the names of four-legged animals that live on a farm. Then have each child make an animal habitat. (See directions on page 188.) *Fine-motor skills*

Wednesday

Program for each child a card with the name of a day of the week. Have each student take a card and read the word to herself. Then name a day and have each student with the matching word stand and face the class. Lead students to greet each other with the chant shown. *Days of the week*

Oink, moo, cock-a-doodle-doo,
Happy [Wednesday] to all of you!
Oink, moo, cock-a-doodle-doo,
Happy [Wednesday] to all of you!

Review fiction and nonfiction story elements. Then show the front cover of *Click, Clack, Moo: Cows That Type* by Doreen Cronin and read aloud the title. Have each youngster predict whether the book would be classified as fiction or nonfiction. Following a read-aloud of the story, discuss student predictions. *Fiction and nonfiction, making predictions*

Thursday

Guide students to name the basic needs of living things (food, water, and shelter). Continue with a discussion that compares and contrasts the basic needs of two different farm animals. Then instruct each child to draw a picture of and write about one of the animals and how one of its needs is met. *Basic needs of animals*

Reread yesterday's story, pausing for students to identify fiction and nonfiction parts of the tale. Then guide students to provide specific examples that support this story's classification as a fictitious tale. *Critical thinking*

Friday

Brainstorm with students different farm animal activities. Then give two-step farm-related oral directions, such as "Oink like a pig and then gallop like a horse." *Following two-step directions*

Choose your favorite version of the story *The Little Red Hen* and share it with your youngsters. Then have each child make a hen craft. (See directions on page 188.) Encourage youngsters to use the completed craft to tell the moral of the story. *Story recall*

Literacy and Math

Discuss with students the different chores a farmer does on a farm. Write each job on a card and use the cards to label the columns of a graphing chart. Then have each youngster place a personalized sticky note in a column to show which job he would like to do. Guide youngsters to use the graph to draw conclusions about each job. **Graphing**

Give each student a yellow pom-pom (chick) and have them sing the song shown. At the song's end, have students position their chicks where desired and freeze. Then select a child to use the correct positional word(s) to complete the sentence "My chick is _____ me."
Positional words

(sung to the tune of "Shoo Fly")
My chick moves all around.
My chick moves all around.
My chick moves all around.
Now ask me where my chick is found!

Draw a simple pig outline on the board and write the rime *-ig* on it. Have a youngster write a letter (or tape a letter card) on the pig and have her read the resulting word. If it is a real word, encourage the remaining students to say, "Oink!" Repeat the process with different letters. **Making new words**

w ig

Give each child a copy of the cow mat on page 189 and eight black paper spots. Have one student roll a large die and announce the number. After each child puts this many spots on his cow, ask him to add one (or two) more. Enlist students' help in writing the corresponding addition sentence. Then have students remove the spots and repeat the activity. **Adding**

Have youngsters share real happenings on a farm, such as feeding the animals, and fictional events with a farm setting, such as cows typing and sheep singing. Then have them draw and label a farm scene that shows a real and an imaginary event happening on a farm. **Real and make-believe**

Song

*(sung to the tune of
"The Farmer in the Dell")*

Down on the farm,
Down on the farm,
We hear the animals
Down on the farm.

We hear the [sheep].
We hear the [sheep].
[Baa, baa, baa, baa, baa, baa,]
We hear the [sheep].

Sing additional verses by replacing the underlined text with the names of different farm animals and their sounds.

Concepts of print: Post the song in a pocket chart. Invite youngsters, in turn, to track the words with a farm-related pointer while the class sings the song.

Journal Prompts

- Draw a farmer doing a chore on a farm. Write about it.

- Draw three ducks walking in a row. Write to tell where the ducks are going.

- Draw a pig in the mud. Write about the pig.

- Draw two farm animals. Write about them.

- Draw yourself working on a farm. Write about what you are doing.

Instructions

Handsome Animal Habitat

Materials for one habitat: 9" x 12" sheet of construction paper (background), 6" x 9" sheet of construction paper, paper scraps, yarn, scissors, glue, crayons

Steps:

1. Trace your hand on the construction paper and cut it out.
2. Glue the hand cutout to your background.
3. Use crayons, yarn, and paper scraps to transform the handprint into a four-legged farm animal.
4. Add details to the scene to create your animal's farm habitat.

Red Hen

Materials for one hen: tagboard cutouts of the hen patterns on page 190, brown and red construction paper, paper scraps, scissors, glue

Steps:

1. Trace the hen body cutout on brown paper. Trace the comb and wattle on red paper.
2. Cut out the tracings. Use paper scraps to make feet, a beak, an eye, and feathers.
3. Glue the pieces together so they resemble a hen.

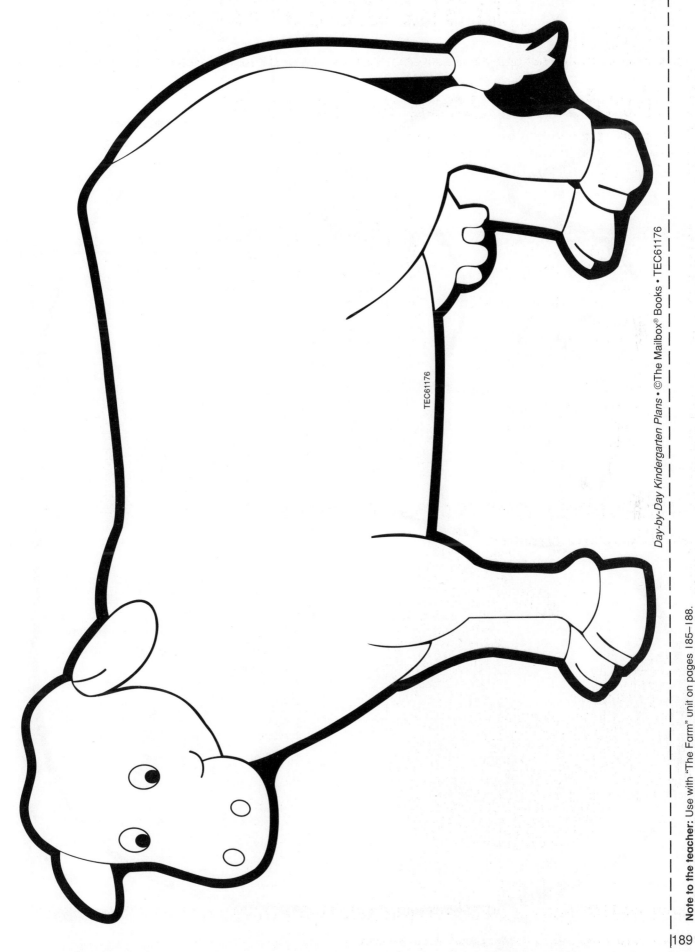

TEC61176

Day-by-Day Kindergarten Plans • ©The Mailbox® Books • TEC61176

Note to the teacher: Use with "The Farm" unit on pages 185–188.

Hen Body, Wattle, and Comb Patterns
Use with the "The Farm" unit on pages 185–188.

TEC61176

Eggs

Centers for the Week

ABC Center: Write different uppercase letters on a supply of plastic eggs. On each of several sterilized egg carton sections, write each matching lowercase letter. A student places each uppercase letter egg in the matching lowercase letter section. *Matching uppercase and lowercase letters*

Reading Center: Program the right half of a plastic egg with a rime. Then, twisting the left half of the egg, write different letters to make words in the word family. A student twists the egg to read the words and then writes on a sheet of paper each word in the word family. *Word families*

Math Center: Store ten plastic eggs in a sanitized egg carton. Place at a center the carton, a die, and blank paper. A child writes the number 10 on his paper. Then he rolls the die, removes the corresponding number of eggs from the carton, and completes the subtraction sentence. *Subtraction*

Writing Center: Set out a supply of large egg cutouts. A child cuts across the center of an egg to create a cracked egg. She glues the two egg pieces to a sheet of construction paper. Then she draws and writes about an imaginary creature that hatched out of the egg. *Creative writing*

Game Center: For this partner game, set out two sterilized egg cartons and six eggs in each of four colors. Player One starts an *AB* pattern across a row of an egg carton. Player Two extends the pattern in the second egg carton. Then the players switch roles to extend a second pattern. *Patterning*

Morning Group Time	Read-Alouds and Art
Monday Have youngsters, in turn, roll a plastic egg filled with play dough to a classmate. Lead students in greeting each child holding the rolled egg with the greeting shown, substituting the second set of letters in parentheses with the same beginning sound as the child's name. **Phonics** Hello, [Charlie]! Have a happy, [ch]appy day!	After reminding students that each person is uniquely special, read aloud *Eggbert, the Slightly Cracked Egg* by Tom Ross. Choose two students and have them stand. Choose another student to tell a way in which the two youngsters are alike and a way in which they are different. ***Character education***
Tuesday Hide several plastic eggs. Then give youngsters clues, one at a time, about where an egg might be found. When the egg's location has been identified correctly, invite one youngster to get the egg. Continue in this manner for each remaining egg. ***Listening skills***	Revisit yesterday's story to discuss how Eggbert's feelings changed throughout the story. Invite each youngster to share a time when he felt like Eggbert. Then have each child make an "Egg-ceptional" Egg Pair. (See directions on page 194.) ***Making connections***
Wednesday Place a desired number of eggs on cellophane grass. Then have each youngster estimate the number of eggs and write the estimate on a sticky note. Lead youngsters in counting the eggs. Then invite each child to post her estimation on a chart similar to the one shown. ***Estimation*** | Under	Actual Number of Eggs	Over		Discuss with students what it means to be responsible and faithful. Then read aloud *Horton Hatches the Egg* by Dr. Seuss. Follow up with a discussion about the repetitive text "I meant what I said and I said what I meant. … An elephant's faithful one hundred [percent]!" ***Vocabulary***
Thursday For each picture card on page 195, help youngsters name the letter of the beginning sound and write it on chart paper. Invite a youngster to write *e* on an egg cutout and tape it to the chart for the short vowel *e*. Then help youngsters name and write the letter(s) to complete the word. ***Short vowel e***	After revisiting yesterday's story, ask students to share what they know about Horton. Have students share what they know about real elephants. List responses on the board. Lead youngsters to determine that the story is make believe. Have volunteers mark out each detail about Horton that is not realistic. ***Real and make-believe***
Friday Brainstorm with students the different ways eggs are cooked. Write each response to make a list. Then use a tally mark to show each student's favorite type of egg. Guide students to use the data to draw conclusions, such as which type of egg is the class favorite. ***Organizing and analyzing data***	**Colorful Egg** *(See directions on page 194.)*  I made blue and yellow stripes. When I mixed the colors, I made green!

Literacy and Math

Have each child color an egg cutout to show a pattern of her choice. Post each completed egg on a display titled "Perfectly Patterned Eggs." Invite each youngster, in turn, to describe her pattern design. ***Patterning***

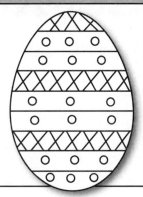

For each of several small groups, program a large egg cutout with a different letter. Have each group cut out from magazines pictures that begin with the letter's sound and glue them on the egg. ***Beginning sounds***

For this small-group activity, gather a supply of plastic eggs and label matching halves with high-frequency words. Hide one half of each egg in the room and place the other half on a table. Have each child search for an egg half. When she finds one, she takes it to the table and attaches it to the matching half. Then she reads the word to you and places it in a basket before searching for another egg half. ***High-frequency words***

Have each youngster sit in one of four rows stemming away from a basket. Instruct youngsters to use spoons to pass different-colored plastic eggs from the end of each row into the basket. After a predetermined amount of time, stop the game. Then help students make a class graph to show how many eggs of each color made it into the basket. ***Gross-motor skills, graphing***

Place a picture of a different object in each of several plastic eggs. (If desired, use the picture cards on page 195.) Invite students, in turn, to open an egg and use words to describe the object until it is named correctly. Continue in this manner with each remaining egg. ***Descriptive language***

Song

(sung to the tune of "Clementine")

On a big farm, in the hen house,
There are lots of eggs to see.
Big and little, fragile ovals,
To be handled carefully.

Vocabulary: Point out the egg descriptors in the third line. Discuss why these words are appropriate to describe eggs. Then have youngsters give reasons to support the last line of the song.

Journal Prompts

- Draw and write about how you might rescue an egg that is falling to the ground.

- Draw and write about a dinosaur egg that has just hatched.

- Draw eggs prepared for breakfast. Write about why you would or would not eat the eggs.

- Draw an animal that lays eggs. Write about it.

- Draw a spotted egg. Write and complete the following sentence: "When my spotted egg hatched, _____."

Instructions

"Egg-ceptional" Egg Pair

Materials for one pair: two white egg cutouts, sheet of construction paper, white crayon, markers, construction paper scraps

Steps:

1. Use the crayon to make white spots on one of the egg cutouts and stripes on the other. Then color both eggs with markers.
2. Place the eggs side by side on your paper. Use construction paper scraps to make facial details, arms, and legs for each egg.
3. Glue the pieces in place to show two egg friends, one with spots and one with stripes, side by side.

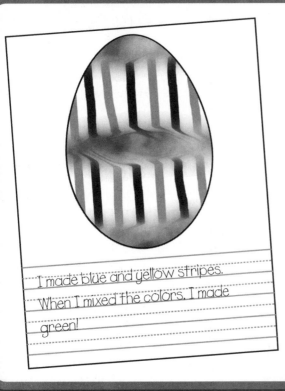

I made blue and yellow stripes. When I mixed the colors, I made green!

Colorful Egg

Materials for one egg: egg cutout; red, blue, and yellow paint in squeeze bottles; paintbrush; story paper; glue; crayons

Steps:

1. Choose two different-colored paints. Squeeze alternating colors of stripes on the egg.
2. Use a paintbrush to blend the colors at the top and bottom of the egg. Then swirl the colors across the center to make a line. Let the paint dry.
3. Write to tell what happened to the colors on the egg. Then glue the egg to the paper. Add details as desired.

TEC61176

TEC61176

TEC61176

TEC61176

TEC61176

TEC61176

TEC61176

TEC61176

TEC61176

TEC61176

TEC61176

TEC61176

Colored Eggs

by _____

Day-by-Day Kindergarten Plans • ©The Mailbox® Books • TEC61176

 +  =

Red   and   yellow   make   orange.   1

  =

Yellow   and   blue   make   green.   2

 +  =

Blue   and   red   make   purple.   3

Note to the teacher: Have each student read each sentence and color the eggs the corresponding colors. Then have him cut apart the pages and staple them in order behind the front cover.

Flowers

Centers for the Week

Writing Center: Program a supply of colorful flower cutouts (patterns on page 201) with clip art or a writing topic. Glue each flower to a craft stick. Then place the flowers in a plastic flowerpot. A child chooses a topic and writes about it in her journal. ***Journal writing***

Reading Center: Glue flower cutouts (patterns on page 201) to craft sticks. Label one flower with a short *a* and program the other flowers with the consonants in chosen consonant-short *a*-consonant words. Insert three flowers in a block of floral foam to make a word. A child reads the word and then copies it onto a sheet of paper. Then he uses the flowers to form and write new words. ***Making new words***

Math Center: Set out two plastic vases, artificial flowers, and a number die. A child rolls the die, places the matching number of flowers in one of the vases, and writes the number on his paper. He repeats this step for the second vase. Then he circles the greater of the two numbers and repeats the activity. ***Comparing sets***

Art Center: Set out shallow containers of paint in different colors, artificial flowers, and paintbrushes. A youngster dips a flower in paint and makes flower prints on a sheet of paper. Then she uses the paintbrush to paint stems and leaves for each flower. ***Painting***

Science Center: Set out copies of the cards on page 201. A child cuts out the cards and glues them in order on a sheet of paper to show the growth of a plant. For an added challenge, he writes to tell about each picture. ***Plant growth***

Morning Group Time	Read-Alouds and Art
Monday Draw on a sheet of chart paper a flower with a stem, leaves, and roots. Help youngsters label the parts of the plant. Then show youngsters an actual flowering plant and encourage them to name its different parts as they did with the drawing. **Flower parts**	Show the front cover and read aloud the title of Lois Ehlert's book *Planting a Rainbow*. Then ask youngsters to predict what the story will be about. After reading the book, lead a discussion about student-made predictions. **Making predictions**
Tuesday Write a different letter on each of several flower cutouts. Scatter the flowers on the floor. Have youngsters sit around the flowers. Give a child an empty watering can and have him pretend to water one of the flowers as he identifies the letter. Then invite his classmates to name words that begin with that letter. **Initial consonants** 	Reread yesterday's story, pausing to discuss vocabulary words such as *bulbs, sprout, seedlings, sow,* and *blooms*. Help youngsters use context clues to develop comprehension of the full text. **Vocabulary and context clues**
Wednesday Place a large bouquet of artificial flowers in a vase. Have each youngster estimate the total number of flowers in the vase and write the number on a sticky note. Then lead youngsters in counting the flowers and invite the child with the closest estimate to rearrange the bouquet. **Estimation**	**Sweet-Smelling Flower** *(See directions on page 200.)* 
Thursday Cut out stems, leaves, and flower heads so there is one flower part per child. (Make sure that when the parts are put together each flower has all the parts.) Give each student a cutout. Then name each part, in turn, and have youngsters with the matching cutout glue it to a length of bulletin board paper. Display the resulting flower patch. **Flower parts**	Read aloud *Flower Garden* by Eve Bunting. Then have youngsters recall each step it took to get the flower garden from the shopping cart to the garden box in the family's home. **Sequencing events**
Friday On chart paper write a flower-related story starter such as "One lovely spring day, I went to my garden and saw…" Invite students to dictate sentences to complete the story. When the story is finished, read it aloud with students. **Shared writing**	**A Handy Flower** *(See directions on page 200.)* 

Literacy and Math

Gather a supply of artificial flowers that vary in length. Give each child in a small group a flower. Instruct group members to work together to order the flowers from shortest to longest. **Ordering lengths**

Write two numbers on the board. Then, on a sheet of paper, have each youngster draw a flower scene to illustrate an addition sentence using those numbers. **Addition**

$3 + 5 = 8$

3   5

Post two flower cutouts without petals and write a different short vowel on each one. Program several petal cutouts with clip art pictures whose names have one of the featured vowel sounds. Invite a volunteer to take a flower, say the word, and repeat its vowel sound. Then have him post the petal on the correct flower. **Short vowels**

Label several seed packets with prices and give each child a supply of imitation coins. Invite a volunteer to choose a packet of seeds that she would like to purchase. Then have each student use her coins to show the appropriate coin amount. After checking for accuracy, invite another child to shop for seeds. **Counting coins**

Announce several words making sure to include several that begin with *fl* like *flower*. Each time a child hears a word that begins like *flower*, he slowly stands and pretends to grow like a flower. Then he sits back down and listens for the next word. **Initial blend fl**

Song

(sung to the tune of "Are You Sleeping?")

Lots of flowers, lots of flowers,
Some are small, some grow tall.
Yellow, pink, and blue,
Orange and red too.
Flowers grow. Flowers grow.

Measurement: Discuss with students that different types of flowers can grow to different heights. Then have youngsters use a ruler to make five flowers increasing in height across a sheet of paper.

Journal Prompts

- Draw a flower that you would like to give to someone. Then write and complete the sentence, "I gave the flower to _____."

- Draw butterflies and bees in a flower scene. Write about them.

- Draw the best garden ever. Write about it.

- Draw a flower head, stem, and leaves. Label each part and then write about the flower.

- Pretend you planted a magic seed. Draw a picture of what grew. Write about it.

Instructions

Sweet-Smelling Flower

Materials for one flower: construction paper flower cutout (if desired, enlarge the pattern on page 201), plastic bag containing colorful loop cereal, glue, scissors

Steps:
1. Cut out the flower.
2. Mash the cereal into smaller pieces.
3. Drizzle a glue design in the center of the flower cutout.
4. Pour the cereal pieces over the glue.
5. When the glue is dry, shake the excess cereal off the flower.

A Handy Flower

Materials for one flower: sheet of construction paper, paper circle, thin paper rectangle (stem), 2 paper ovals (leaves), paint, pencil, scissors, glue

Steps:
1. Coat your hand with paint and make five handprints on your paper.
2. Use a pencil to draw an outline around each print to make petal shapes. Cut out each shape.
3. Glue the petals to the circle.
4. Glue the resulting flower and leaves to the stem.

Flower Patterns and Sequencing Cards

Use with the "Flowers" unit on pages 197–200.

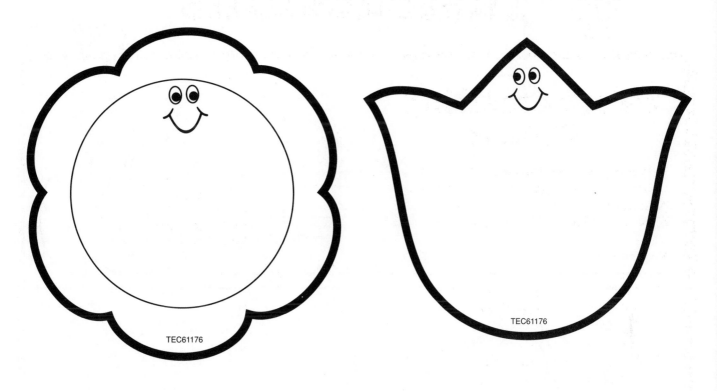

Name_____

Beautiful Blossoms

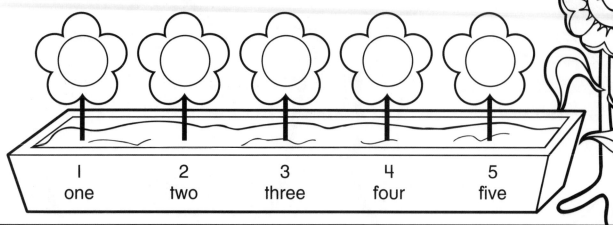

Read and do.

l	2	3	4	5
one	two	three	four	five

Color two flowers red.
Color one flower blue.

Color four flowers orange.
Color three flowers yellow.

Color five flowers purple.
Color one flower pink.

Draw two yellow flowers.
Draw three red flowers.

Day-by-Day Kindergarten Plans • ©The Mailbox® Books • TEC61176

Caterpillars and Butterflies

Centers for the Week

ABC Center: Cut out ten copies of the butterfly pattern on page 207. Place a different sticker on each left wing. Write the matching letter(s) for each sticker's final consonant sound on the right wing. Then cut off the right wings. A student names each sticker and places the wing with the corresponding ending sound on the butterfly. *Final consonants*

Writing Center: Set out a class supply of copies of the butterfly pattern from page 207. A child colors and cuts out a butterfly. Next, he folds the wings forward and glues the body to the top of a sheet of story paper, leaving the wings free. Then he writes about an imaginary experience with the butterfly. *Story writing*

Math Center: Provide blank paper, two or three different-color ink pads, and markers. A student makes a fingerprint pattern to form a colorful caterpillar body. Then he uses the markers to draw facial details and legs. He repeats the activity, making different patterns. *Patterns*

Art Center: Set out enlarged construction paper copies of the butterfly pattern on page 207 and two to three squirt bottles of paint in contrasting colors. A child cuts out a butterfly and folds it in half. Next, he opens the butterfly and squirts two or three colors of paint into the fold. After refolding the paper, he rubs the outside to blend the paint. Then he unfolds the paper and takes notice of the resulting symmetrical design. *Symmetry*

Fine-Motor Center: Provide different circular items—such as film containers, plastic spools, and milk jug lids—for students to trace. A child traces the objects side by side to create a caterpillar. Then he colors the critter as desired and uses a marker to add facial details and legs. *Tracing, coloring*

Morning Group Time	Read-Alouds and Art
Monday Give each student a copy of a caterpillar or butterfly card from page 207. Then say a word that begins with /b/ or /k/. If the child's critter has the same beginning sound as the word, he flutters or crawls like the critter on his card. If not, he freezes until the next word is called. ***Beginning sounds***	Read aloud a nonfiction book, such as *From Caterpillar to Butterfly* by Deborah Heiligman, about the life cycle of a butterfly. Then have each child complete "Butterfly Life Cycle." (See directions on page 206.) ***Life cycle of a butterfly***
Tuesday Give each child a butterfly cutout (see page 207 for a pattern) labeled with a different number in a series. Place a length of tape on the floor. Announce the first number in the number series. The child holding that number flutters like a butterfly to place his cutout on the tape line. Students continue placing the butterflies in numerical order. ***Number order*** 	Revisit the pages of yesterday's story that tell what a caterpillar eats. Then read aloud *The Very Hungry Caterpillar* by Eric Carle. Follow up with a discussion about the elements of each book that make it fiction or nonfiction. ***Fiction and nonfiction***
Wednesday Place a copy of a caterpillar card and a butterfly card (see page 207) at the top of a pocket chart. Have students clap the number of syllables per word as you label a blank card with the corresponding number of syllables. Then sort pictures of three- or four-syllable words under the corresponding headings. ***Syllables*** 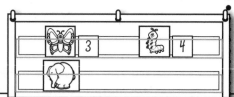	Revisit yesterday's story. Then enlist students' help in creating a graph to show the number of foods eaten each day. Have students use the graph to answer questions such as "Did the caterpillar eat more food on weekdays or on the weekend?" ***Graphing***
Thursday Give each child a butterfly cutout (pattern on page 207), each labeled with a different number. Then ask questions, such as "Who has a number that is less than five?" and "Who has a number that is greater than 17?" and have students hold up their butterflies to respond. ***Comparing numbers***	**Beautiful Butterfly** *(See directions on page 206.)* 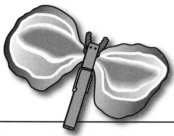
Friday After discussing butterfly metamorphosis with students, announce true and false sentences about the topic. Instruct students to say, "Munch, crunch" for each true statement. If the statement is false, have each student curl up in a ball as if she were in a chrysalis. ***True and false, living things***	Read *Charlie the Caterpillar* by Dom Deluise. Lead youngsters in describing how Charlie's feelings change throughout the story. ***Story recall***

Literacy and Math

After familiarizing youngsters with the rhyme below, have each child draw the number of butterflies first mentioned. Direct him to cross out butterflies to show how many fly away. Then have him write the matching subtraction sentence. Repeat with other numbers.
Subtraction

<u>6</u> *butterflies are way up high.*
<u>2</u> *fly away, high into the sky.*

Write "caterpillar" and "butterfly" on separate cards. Then cover the initial letter of each word with a different letter. Ask youngsters to read aloud each new nonsense word. Continue with different letters as time permits.
Beginning sounds

Label two paper circles each with a different short vowel. Add eyes, a mouth, and antennae to each cutout. Program additional circles with pictures whose names contain the vowel sounds. Scramble the circles. Then have students, in turn, place the circles side by side to form caterpillars. ***Short-vowel words***

Write a compound word on each butterfly cutout in a class supply (enlarge the pattern on page 207); then cut each butterfly in half. Post one half of each butterfly in a pocket chart and stack the other cutouts nearby. Read the words in the pocket chart. Then take a cutout from the stack and read the word aloud. Invite a volunteer to "fly" the butterfly to the chart and make a match. ***Compound words***

Show students a collection of nine green pom-poms (caterpillars) and one white pom-pom (egg) before putting the pom-poms in a paper bag. Then invite volunteers, in turn, to remove a caterpillar or an egg at random. Lead students to conclude that a caterpillar is more likely to be picked and help them explain why.
Probability

Song

(sung to the tune of
"Are You Sleeping?")

Caterpillars
Spin cocoons
And stay inside,
Where they hide.
When they're ready, they push out.
With new wings they fly about,
Through the sky,
Way up high.

Science: After singing the song, ask youngsters to identify the insect (butterfly) inferred that will *push out,* has *new wings,* and can *fly about.*
Making inferences

Journal Prompts

- Draw a hungry caterpillar. Write about what it will eat.

- Draw two different butterflies. Write about them.

- Imagine you could change into something as a caterpillar does. Draw and write about what you would like to change into. Tell why.

- Draw a butterfly flying over your favorite place. Write about what it sees.

- Draw and write about how you would take care of a pet caterpillar.

Instructions

Beautiful Butterfly

Materials for one butterfly: clothespin, coffee filter, bowls of tinted water in different colors, small length of pipe cleaner, markers

Steps:
1. Fold the filter in half. Keeping it folded, make more folds as desired and dip opposing edges in different bowls. Carefully unfold the filter and let it dry.
2. To make antennae, twist the pipe cleaner around one side of the clip end of the clothespin.
3. Gather the filter in the center and clip the clothespin to the filter to hold it in place. Gently spread the wings.
4. Use the marker to draw eyes on the tip of the clothespin.

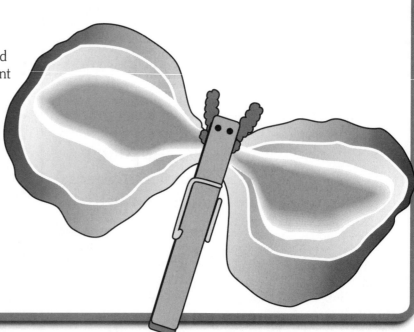

Butterfly Life Cycle

Materials for one life cycle: paper plate, small white pom-pom (egg), spiral noodle (caterpillar), shell noodle (pupa), bowtie noodle (butterfly), brown length of pipe cleaner (branch), two green leaf cutouts, markers, glue

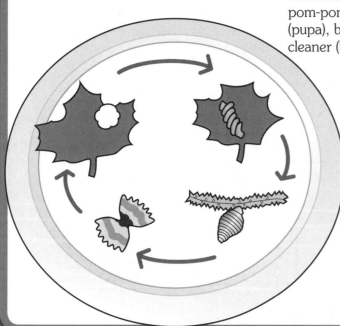

Steps:
1. Glue the egg to a leaf.
2. Color the caterpillar green and glue it to the other leaf. Tear parts of the leaf to represent the caterpillar's munched path.
3. Color the pupa brown.
4. Color the butterfly's wings.
5. Glue the pieces in order on the plate. Glue the branch above the pupa.
6. Draw arrows to show the sequence of the cycle.

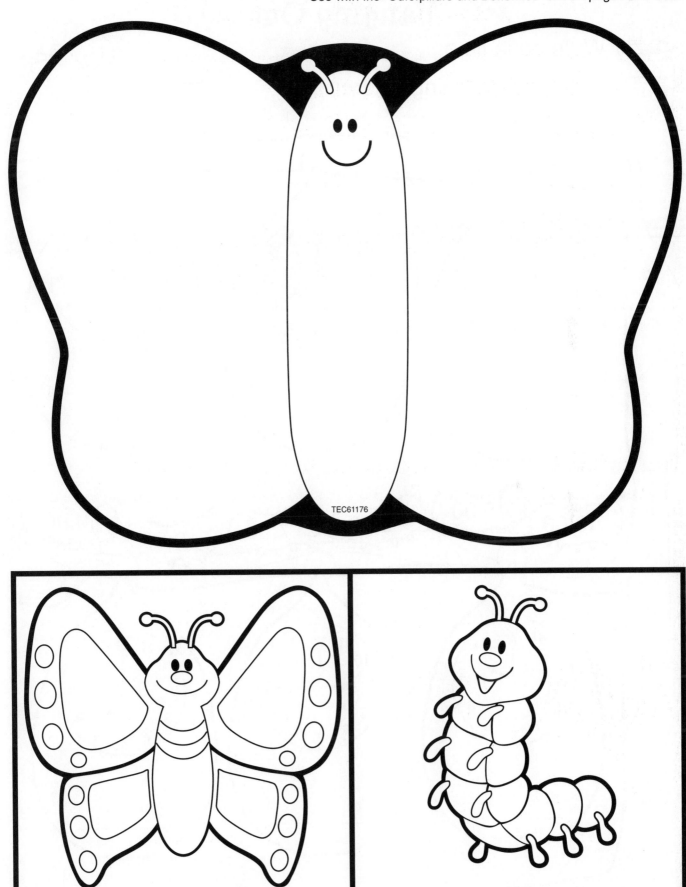

TEC61176

TEC61176

TEC61176

Hanging Out

✏️ Write each time.

🖍️ Color the matching caterpillar.

___ : ___

___ : ___

___ : ___

10:00   5:00   2:00   7:00   9:00   4:00

___ : ___

___ : ___

___ : ___

Day-by-Day Kindergarten Plans • ©The Mailbox® Books • TEC61176

More Insects!

Centers for the Week

Writing Center: Post lists of color, size, number, and shape words. A youngster draws and colors on a sheet of story paper an insect with three body parts and six legs. Then she uses the words on the lists as she writes to describe her creation. *Descriptive words*

Reading Center: Make a class supply of copies of the sentence strips on page 213. A student cuts out the strips, glues each sentence on an individual half sheet of paper, and illustrates each one. When the glue is dry, he staples the pages behind a cover and reads his buggy booklet. *Reading sentences*

Math Center: Set out ten leaf cutouts and 20 red pom-poms (ladybugs). A student puts two ladybugs on each leaf. Then she uses the ladybugs to count by twos to 20. *Counting by twos*

Game Center: Set out a hive cutout labeled with numbers from 0 to 10, two sets of shuffled number cards from 0 to 5, and six yellow pom-poms (bees). Each player, in turn, takes two cards, adds the numbers, and places a bee on the matching number on the hive. *Addition*

Science Center: Set out a class supply of copies of the sorting cards from page 213. A student cuts out a copy of the cards and glues the header cards to the top of another sheet of paper. Then he sorts the cards under the corresponding headers and glues them in place. *Insects and noninsects*

Morning Group Time	Read-Alouds and Art
Monday	
Write your morning message using incorrect punctuation marks and missing capital letters. As you reread the message, have volunteers take turns using a flyswatter to swat the errors. Then enlist students' help in correcting the errors. ***Capitalization, punctuation***	Ask students if they think the life of an ant is important. Then read aloud *Hey, Little Ant* by Phillip and Hannah Hoose. Discuss with students any changes in their perception as a result of reading the book. ***Critical thinking***
Tuesday	
Write each number set from *0–7, 8–14, 15–22,* and *23–30* on individual beehive cutouts and place a hive in each of four corners of your room. Give each student a number card with a different number from 0 to 30. Then ask her to buzz like a bee to the corner that corresponds with the number on her card. ***Number order***	After rereading yesterday's story, invite each youngster, in turn, to answer the author's question, "What do you think that kid should do?" ***Point of view***
Wednesday	
Congratulate students for being as busy as bees this school year. Ask youngsters to share what they think the phrase means. Then explain that honey bees have many chores, such as building the honeycomb of wax, guarding the hive, and collecting a sticky substance from trees. Next, have students share their accomplishments as you list their responses on a chart titled "[Teacher's name]'s students have been as busy as bees this year!" ***Self-awareness***	Read aloud *The Grouchy Ladybug* by Eric Carle. After having students recall each of the grouchy ladybug's encounters, help each child make a "Lovely Ladybug" (see directions on page 212). ***Story recall***
Thursday	
Draw a leaf on the board and then draw several simple bugs on the leaf. Explain that the bugs are eating the leaf. Then ask students questions such as the following: "What letter comes before *L?* What is the ending sound of *bug?* What month comes after May?" Erase a bug for each question youngsters answer correctly. ***Review***	Revisit yesterday's story and call attention to the ladybugs' aphid feast at the beginning and end of the book. Discuss with youngsters how some insects are helpful to plants in the real world. Then lead youngsters to explain why the leaf thanked the ladybugs in the story. ***Making connections***
Friday	
Invite youngsters to pretend to be grasshoppers that hop when ready to share an answer. Then give individual clues about a particular insect. When a child thinks he can name the mystery insect, he hops like a grasshopper. Continue with different mystery insect clues as time permits. ***Listening skills***	**Helpful Insects** *(See directions on page 212.)*

Literacy and Math

Draw a leaf on the board and make a supply of ladybug cutouts (patterns on page 213). Show students a ladybug and then have them estimate how many ladybugs will fit on the leaf without overlapping. Have each child write her estimate on a sticky note. Then lead students in counting as you tape the bugs on the leaf. Have students compare their estimates to the actual number. **Estimation**

Give each child a hive cutout that you have programmed with a different set of letters. As you call out a letter's sound, have youngsters use pieces of honeycomb-shaped cereal or counters to cover the corresponding letters on the hives. The first child to cover all his letters wins. **Letter-sound association**

Have each youngster glue a small black paper circle to a larger red paper circle to make a ladybug. Then have her place a desired number of sticky dots (spots) on each wing. Help her write an addition sentence so that the number of spots on the left wing is the first addend and the number of spots on the right wing is the second addend. **Addition**

Write several high-frequency words on the board. Then say one of the words and invite a youngster to swat the word with a flyswatter. Continue with different words and other students. **High-frequency words**

Program each of two construction paper ladybugs with a different ending consonant. Program each of several semicircles (wings) with a sticker whose name ends with one of the letters. Have students match the semicircles with the ladybugs. **Ending sounds**

Song

(sung to the tune of "The More We Get Together")

Oh, let's count a dozen insects.
That's 12 bugs, yes, 12 bugs.
Oh, let's count a dozen insects.
Twelve bugs, here we go.
1, 2, 3, 4, 5, 6,
7, 8, 9, 10, 11, 12.
That's a dozen little insects
We counted, we know.

Vocabulary: Discuss with youngsters the meaning of the word *dozen* and the context clues in the song that tell the word's meaning.

Journal Prompts

- Draw big and little ants. Write about them.

- Draw an insect and a hungry frog. Write about how the insect escapes from the frog.

- Draw and write about a day in the life of an insect.

- Draw a ladybug and a butterfly. Write about how they are the same and how they are different.

- Imagine you could be an insect for a day. Draw and write about the kind of insect you would be and where you would go.

Instructions

Lovely Ladybug

Materials for one ladybug: paper bowl; 6 black paper strips (legs); black paper circles—1 large (head), several small (spots); construction paper scraps; red paint; paintbrush; glue; black marker; scissors

Steps:

1. Paint the outside of the bowl (body).
2. When the paint is dry, draw a line dividing the body in half.
3. Cut facial features and antennae from the paper scraps and glue them to the head.
4. Glue the head, spots, and legs to the body.

Bees help flowers.

Helpful Insects

Materials for one helpful insect craft: 9" x 12" construction paper sheet, green leaf cutouts, 3 sticky dots (seed pods), 18 pom-poms (flower petals), 3 pipe cleaners (flower stems), ink pad, markers, glue

Steps:

1. Arrange the flower parts on your paper to make three flowers and glue them in place.
2. Make three connected fingerprints to create a body for each of several insects. Draw wings, six legs, and antennae on each insect. Add desired details.
3. Write a sentence about your drawing.

Sentence Strips, Sorting Cards, and Ladybug Patterns

Use with the "More Insects!" unit on pages 209–212.

The red insect is little. TEC61176	The orange insect is big.
The blue insect is spotted.	The yellow insect has wings.

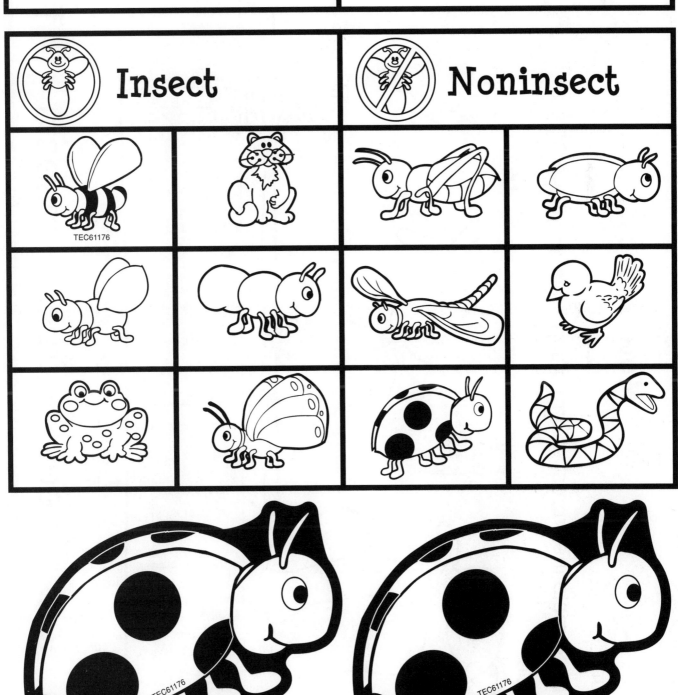

More Insects!

Unscramble the words to form a sentence.

 Cut.

 Glue.

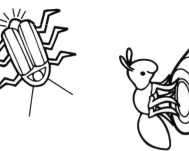

ten	sees	frog	insects.	The

Pond Life

Centers for the Week

ABC Center: Write a different consonant on each of several craft foam lily pads and place them in a large tub of water. Spray-paint a few table tennis balls green (frogs). A student drops a frog on a lily pad and then names the letter on the pad and a word that begins with that letter's sound. ***Letter-sound association***

Reading Center: Prepare a personalized headband for each student by attaching two large paper eyes to a green paper strip and stapling the ends of the strip together. Set out the headbands along with a supply of pond-themed books. Also place a blue blanket on the floor to represent water and add a few green pillows for lily pads. A student puts on her headband and reads one or more of the books. ***Reading***

Writing Center: Post at the center a copy of the pond animal cards on page 219. A student chooses an animal to write about. He then writes facts or a story about the animal. ***Writing***

Math Center: Set out addition and subtraction flash cards, a large paper log, and ten frog counter cards (page 220). A student manipulates the frogs on the log to determine the answer to each problem. ***Adding, subtracting***

Art Center: A student sponge-paints a paper plate half blue. Then she glues thin green paper strips (grass) along the straight edge of the plate half. Next, she uses paper scraps to make desired pond animals and glues them to her pond. ***Artistic expression***

Morning Group Time	Read-Alouds and Art
Monday Put water, seeds, grass, and small plastic insects in a disposable pie pan and place the pan in the freezer until the water is solid. Show students the frozen water and explain that many ponds freeze during the winter, making it difficult for the ducks to get food. Then explain that in winter, many ducks migrate to warmer areas. *Investigating living things*	Show students the cover of *Jump, Frog, Jump!* by Robert Kalen and read the title. Instruct students to study the cover and discuss why the author titled the book *Jump, Frog, Jump!* Read the book aloud. *Drawing conclusions*

Monday

Put water, seeds, grass, and small plastic insects in a disposable pie pan and place the pan in the freezer until the water is solid. Show students the frozen water and explain that many ponds freeze during the winter, making it difficult for the ducks to get food. Then explain that in winter, many ducks migrate to warmer areas. *Investigating living things*

Show students the cover of *Jump, Frog, Jump!* by Robert Kalen and read the title. Instruct students to study the cover and discuss why the author titled the book *Jump, Frog, Jump!* Read the book aloud. *Drawing conclusions*

Tuesday

Write each alphabet letter on a separate lily pad cutout and arrange the pads in a circle on the floor. During the activity, start and stop a selection of lively music. While the music plays, students hop around the circle of lily pads. When the music stops, each child quickly hops onto a lily pad and, in turn, identifies the letter on her cutout and a word that begins with that letter's sound. *Letter-sound associations*

In yesterday's book, the frog jumps away from danger. Have students brainstorm other ways to move. Then have each child draw a frog doing a desired movement and help him write a sentence like the one shown. *Action words*

Spin, frog, spin!

Wednesday

Remind youngsters that, like other animals, frogs grow and change. Give each pair of students a set of the life cycle cards on page 220. Instruct the partners to order the cards to show how a frog grows and changes. Invite volunteers to explain the order. *Life cycles*

Ribbit! Ribbit!
(See directions on page 218.)

Thursday

Place three hoops (ponds) on the floor in separate areas of the classroom. Label each hoop with a different rime. Program a class supply of duck cutouts so each has a word with a featured rime. Give each child a duck and have him place it in the corresponding pond. Then collect the ducks and redistribute them to play again. *Word families*

Show students the cover of *One Duck Stuck* by Phyllis Root and read the title. Invite students to brainstorm how Duck might get out of the mud. Read the story aloud. Then lead students in comparing their ideas to what happens in the story. *Making predictions*

Friday

On the board, draw a T chart and label the columns "Alike" and "Different." Post two cards from page 219. Invite students to name similarities and differences between the animals as you write their responses on the chart. Repeat the activity with different pond animals. *Comparing*

Bucky the Beaver
(See directions on page 218.)

Literacy and Math

Draw several lily pads on a sheet of paper and label each pad with a different letter. Give each child a copy of the page and a supply of green pom-poms (frogs). To call a letter, say a word that begins with the letter. Each student places a pom-pom on the corresponding lily pad. **Letter-sound association**

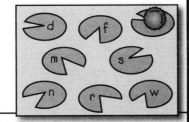

Give each student a pond cutout and ten fish-shaped crackers. Write a number word on the board. Have each child read the word and put the corresponding number of fish on her pond. **Number words**

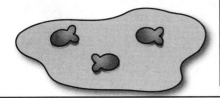

three

Cut apart several copies of the animal cards on page 219. Use the cards to start a pattern and then ask a student to add the next card. Continue inviting students to add to the pattern until it has repeated three times. Use different patterns to repeat the activity. **Patterning**

Label each of three large paper logs with a different rime. Program several frog cutouts with words that have the featured rimes. Have students help sort the frogs onto the correct logs. Then have the class read each group of words. **Word families**

In a paved play area, mark a line ten feet in length for each of several small groups. Tell students that some frogs can jump ten feet or more. Have each child, in turn, stand at one end of the line and count the number of jumps it takes for him to jump the length of the line. Then have the group members compare their numbers of jumps. **Measurement**

Song

(sung to the tune of "Do Your Ears Hang Low?")

There are many things
In a pond for you to find,
Like some tadpoles and
Slippery frogs of every kind.
You'll find cattails there
And some lily pads that grew.
There are big fish too.

Plural words: Display a copy of the song and enlist students' help in circling the plural words.

Journal Prompts

- Draw yourself sitting beside a pond. Write about what you might see there.

- Draw your favorite pond animal. Write about why it is your favorite.

- Write and complete the following sentence: "Once I went fishing and caught a _____." Illustrate your sentence.

- Draw a mother duck with her ducklings. Write about what they are doing.

- Write about what you would do if you met a talking frog. Illustrate your writing.

Instructions

Ribbit! Ribbit!

Materials for one frog: small paper plate, red tagboard strip, construction paper scraps, plastic fly, glue, crayons, scissors, tape

Steps:
1. Use a green crayon to color both sides of the plate. Fold the plate in half.
2. Cut out white paper eyes and color a black circle on each. Glue the eyes to the plate near the fold.
3. Cut out green paper legs and glue them to the back of the plate as shown.
4. Trim the tagboard strip to resemble a tongue and glue the fly to one end of the tongue. Tape the tongue to the inside of the plate.

Bucky the Beaver

Materials for one beaver: 2 brown beaver cutouts (pattern on page 220), smaller tan beaver cutout (reduce the pattern on page 220), 2 small brown paper circles, white paper scraps, 3 round toothpicks, black marker, glue, scissors

Steps:
1. Draw a grid pattern on the tan cutout. Glue the cutout to one of the brown cutouts to make the beaver's tail.
2. To make the beaver's body, glue the circles (ears) on the rounded end of the remaining brown cutout.
3. On the same cutout, draw two eyes, a nose, and a mouth. Glue the toothpicks below the mouth.
4. Cut two teeth from the white paper scraps and glue them on top of the toothpicks.
5. Glue the body and the tail together as shown.

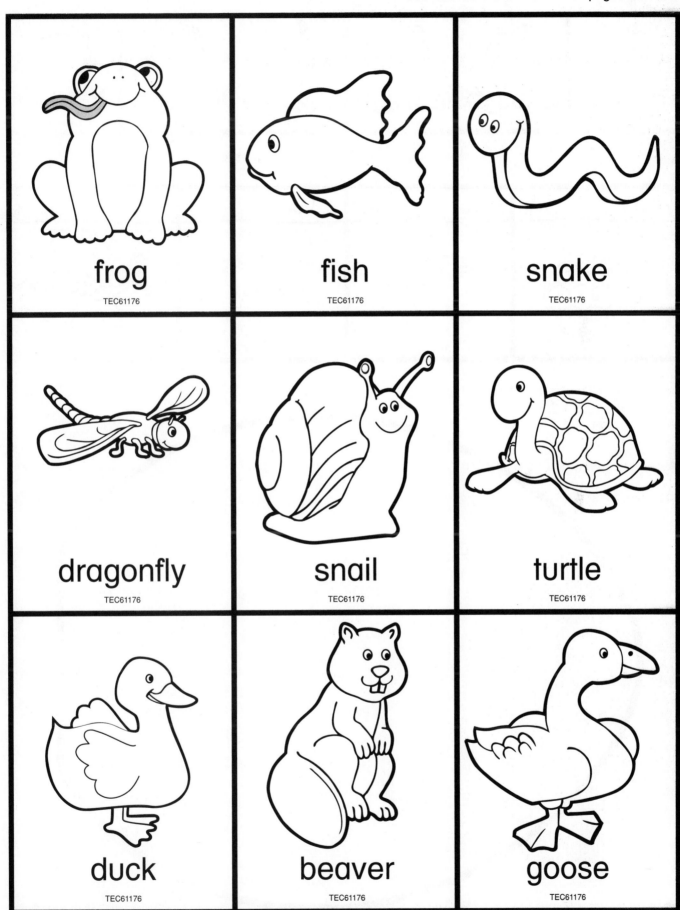

frog
TEC61176

fish
TEC61176

snake
TEC61176

dragonfly
TEC61176

snail
TEC61176

turtle
TEC61176

duck
TEC61176

beaver
TEC61176

goose
TEC61176

Frog Counter Cards, Frog Life Cycle Cards, and Beaver Pattern

Use with the "Pond Life" unit on pages 215–218.

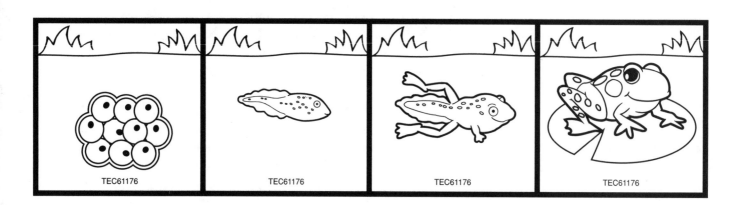

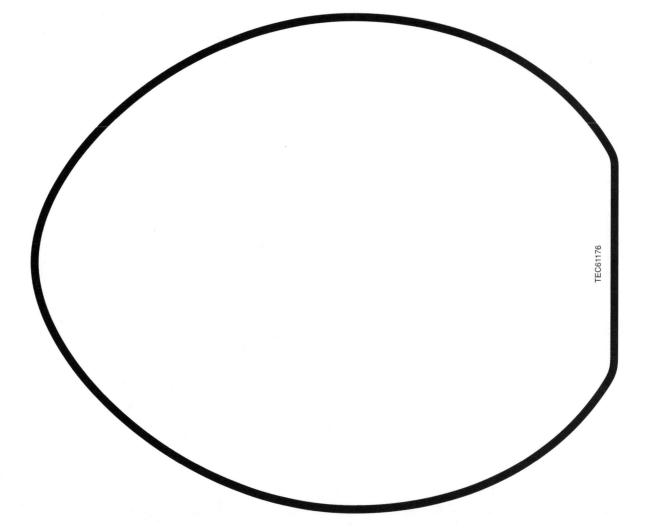

Day-by-Day Kindergarten Plans • ©The Mailbox® Books • TEC61176

Ocean

Centers for the Week

Reading Center: Write high-frequency words on a supply of shell cutouts (pattern on page 225) and then laminate the shells. Bury the shells in a large tub of sand and set plastic digging tools nearby. A student digs up the shells and reads the word on each one. *High-frequency words*

Writing Center: Post a list of beach or ocean words with matching pictures. Supply large beach-themed cutouts, such as a whale, a starfish, or a pail. A student chooses a cutout and uses the word bank to write a story about a day at the beach. *Writing*

Math Center: Set out a tub of sand, a measuring cup, and empty containers, such as a water bottle, a cup, and different-size pails. A student orders the containers from the one he thinks holds the least to the one he thinks holds the most. Then he checks the order by counting the scoops as he scoops sand into each container. *Capacity*

Art Center: Provide a supply of shells, sand, and diluted glue. On a large sheet of paper, a student makes several shell tracings and then colors the tracings. Next, she paints diluted glue around the tracings and sprinkles sand on the glue. *Tracing, coloring, painting*

Science Center: Set out a variety of seashells, magnifying glasses, and balance scales. A student chooses two shells and uses a magnifying glass to compare the shells' features. Then she uses the scales to compare the shells' weights. *Observation, weight*

Morning Group Time	Read-Alouds and Art
Monday Write a different number on each fish in a class supply of fish cutouts (patterns on page 231). Place the fish in a net and have students pass the net around a circle. When a child receives the net, she takes a fish and says, "When I went swimming in the deep blue sea, I saw [number] fish swim by me." **Number recognition**	Show students the front covers of *Octopuses* by Carol K. Lindeen and *My Very Own Octopus* by Bernard Most. Read each title. Have students decide which book is fiction and which book is nonfiction and share their reasoning. Then read aloud *Octopuses*. **Distinguishing fiction from nonfiction**
Tuesday Place a raw egg in a clear container holding two cups of water. Show students that the egg sinks. Remove the egg and add one cup of salt to the water. Tell students that this water is similar to seawater—they both contain salt. Then have youngsters predict whether the egg will still sink when it is placed in the saltwater. Demonstrate that the egg floats in saltwater but not in freshwater. **Properties of matter**	Read aloud *My Very Own Octopus* by Bernard Most and then revisit yesterday's book, *Octopuses*. Lead youngsters in using a Venn diagram to compare real octopuses to the one in today's story. **Using a graphic organizer**
Wednesday Put a supply of shells in a sand pail. Have students sit in a circle and pass the pail to a child. Instruct him to take a shell and name two words to describe his shell. Then have him return the shell to the pail and pass the pail to the next student. Continue until each student has had a turn. **Descriptive words**	**Shapely Octopus** *(See directions on page 224.)*
Thursday Take students to a paved area and mark a length of 25 feet with chalk. Explain that blue whales are about this length when they are born. Help students measure the length with a variety of nonstandard units. Then invite students to compare the length of a newborn blue whale to other animals and objects. **Investigating living things, nonstandard measurement**	Read aloud *Swimmy* by Leo Lionni. Discuss with students how Swimmy helps the school of little red fish. Then invite students to share a time when they helped a friend or relative solve a problem. **Making connections**
Friday Write high-frequency words in random areas on a beach ball. Sit with students in a circle and gently roll the ball to a child. The youngster who catches the ball announces the word that is closest to his right thumb. Then he rolls the ball to a classmate to continue the activity. **High-frequency words**	**Ocean View** *(See directions on page 224.)* 

Literacy and Math

Give each child five small shell cutouts (patterns on page 225). Say a word, emphasizing each sound. As each child repeats the word, have him place one shell per sound on his work area. For example, a student would use three shells for *fish* since it has three sounds. After confirming the number of sounds, have students clear their mats to prepare for the next word. ***Phonological awareness***

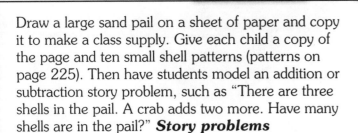

Beach has three sounds.

Draw a large sand pail on a sheet of paper and copy it to make a class supply. Give each child a copy of the page and ten small shell patterns (patterns on page 225). Then have students model an addition or subtraction story problem, such as "There are three shells in the pail. A crab adds two more. Have many shells are in the pail?" ***Story problems***

Decorate a tissue box to look like a shark as shown. Set a bowl containing fish-shaped crackers near the shark. Announce words, some beginning with /sh/. Each time a child hears a word that begins like *shark,* he puts his hands together so they resemble a fin. Then invite a child to "feed" the shark a cracker. ***Digraphs***

Write a different rime on each of three whale cutouts (pattern on page 225). Write words that include the rimes on a supply of cards. Post the whales on the board and draw water above each whale's blowhole. Have students tape the words above the appropriate whale. ***Word families***

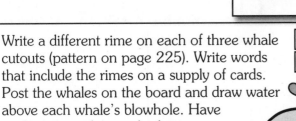

like

hike

-ike

On the board, draw a wavy line to represent an ocean and use Sticky-Tac to attach ten fish cutouts. Invite a student to arrange the fish into two groups. Have each student write the corresponding number sentence on a sheet of paper. After checking for accuracy, repeat the activity using a different grouping of the fish. ***Writing number sentences***

Song

(sung to the tune of "Hush, Little Baby")

The ocean is so big and wide.
Many things live down deep inside.
Like dolphins with their flipping tails
And slowly moving giant whales.
There's seaweed on the ocean floor
And coral reefs and so much more.

High-frequency words: Display a copy of the song. Invite volunteers to find and circle high-frequency words.

Journal Prompts

- Imagine you have discovered a new ocean creature. Draw a picture of the creature and write to describe it.

- Draw your favorite beach activity. Write about why it is your favorite.

- Imagine you are a deep-sea diver. Write about what you might see in the ocean. Illustrate your writing.

- Draw your favorite ocean creature. Write about why it is your favorite.

- Write and complete the following sentence starter: "If I could swim like a fish…" Illustrate your writing.

Instructions

Shapely Octopus

Materials for one octopus: large paper shape (square, circle, triangle, or rectangle), 2 small white circles, eight 12" crepe paper strips, markers, glue

Steps:

1. To make eyes, color a black circle on each white circle. Then glue the circles on the large shape (head).
2. Draw other desired details on the octopus's head.
3. Glue the crepe paper strips along the bottom half of the shape to make tentacles.

Ocean View

Materials for one project: 2 paper plates (1 with the center cut out), clear plastic wrap cut a little larger than the center of a paper plate, foam ocean creatures, paper scraps, sand, diluted glue, glue, paintbrush, scissors, crayons

Steps:

1. Glue the plastic wrap to the inside of the plate with the center missing. Set the plate aside.
2. On the center of the other plate, color the top half blue and paint diluted glue over the bottom half. Sprinkle sand over the glue and shake off the excess sand.
3. Tear or cut the paper scraps to make desired underwater details.
4. Glue the details and the foam creatures on the ocean scene.
5. Glue the inside edges of the two plates together.

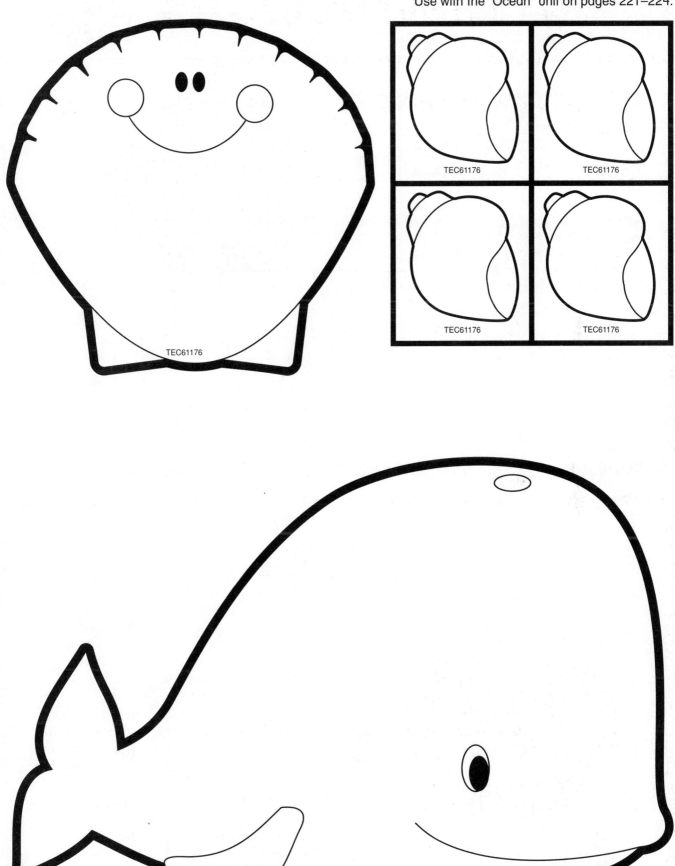

TEC61176

TEC61176

TEC61176

TEC61176

TEC61176

TEC61176

Busy Builders

Cut.

Glue to make word families.

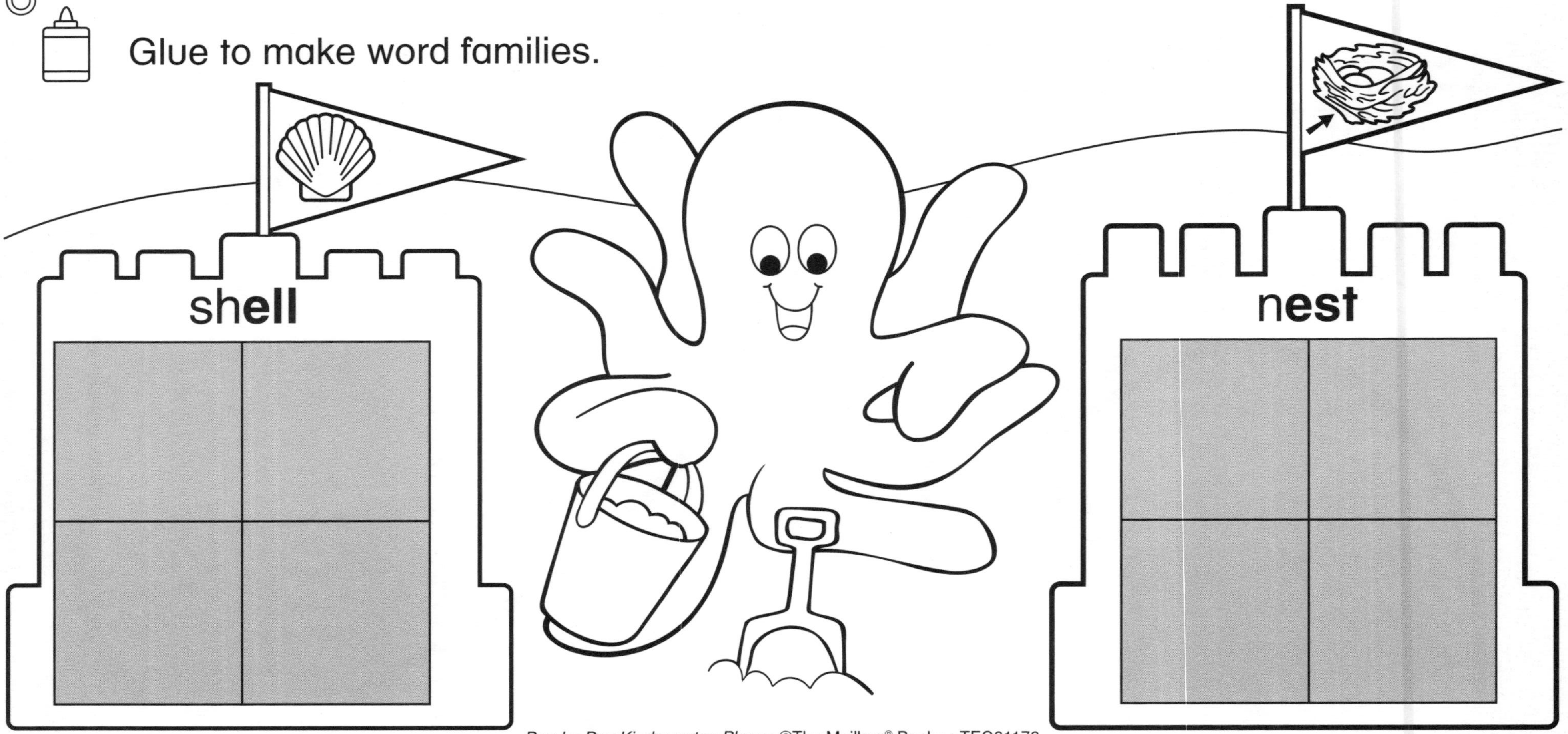

nest

shell

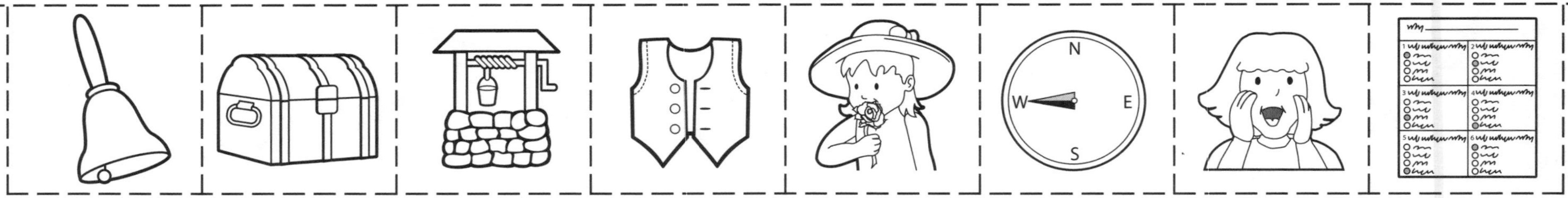

Camping

Centers for the Week

Reading Center: Write a different rime on each card in a supply of light brown cards (graham crackers). Program marshmallow cutouts with onsets, ensuring that some onsets form real words with the rimes and some do not. A student chooses a cracker and puts a marshmallow in front of the cracker. He reads the resulting word and, if it is a real word, writes it on his paper. ***Blending onsets and rimes***

Writing Center: Post a list of camping words and matching pictures. A child uses some of the posted words to write about a camping trip he has taken or a camping trip he would like to take. Then he illustrates his writing. ***Writing***

Math Center: Set out a supply of plastic fishing worms and several items whose lengths can be easily measured. A student places the worms end to end to measure the length of each item. ***Nonstandard measurement***

Art Center: A youngster tears brown paper into strips (logs) and glues the logs to a sheet of blank paper. Then he tears yellow and orange tissue paper into small pieces and glues them on and above the logs so the paper pieces and logs resemble a campfire. ***Tearing***

Science Center: Set out a supply of objects—such as leaves, sticks, and rocks—along with magnifying glasses. A student uses a magnifying glass to observe the similarities and differences of the objects. ***Observation***

Morning Group Time	Read-Alouds and Art
Monday Display several camping-related items and invite students to help explain what they are used for. Then place the items in a backpack. Zip the backpack, leaving an opening large enough for a child's hand to fit inside. In turn, invite students to reach into the backpack, feel an object, and then identify what the item is. **Tactile discrimination**	Show students the cover and read the title of *A Camping Spree With Mr. Magee* by Chris Van Dusen. On the board, draw the outline of a camper similar to the one on the cover. Invite students to name things Mr. Magee might need on his camping trip; write their suggestions on the camper. Then read the book aloud. **Prior knowledge**
Tuesday Program a supply of worm cutouts with high-frequency words. Hide the worms around the room. Instruct each student to find a worm and return to the group-time area. Then, have her read her word aloud. After each student has had a turn, collect the worms and hide them again. **High-frequency words**	Revisit the part of yesterday's story when the camper rolls to a stop beside the car and Mr. Magee and Dee decide to go home. Then have each student write about and illustrate what he would have done if he were Mr. Magee. **Making connections**
Wednesday Dim the lights and sit in a circle with your students. Hold a flashlight and say, "One day, I packed my camping gear and headed for the woods." Hand the flashlight to a student beside you and instruct him to add to your story. Continue around the circle until the flashlight returns to you. Then add an ending. **Oral language**	Read aloud Margaret and H. A. Rey's *Curious George Goes Camping*. Post three bucket cutouts labeled "beginning," "middle," and "end." Ask students to name events that take place at the beginning of the story and write these on the corresponding bucket. Repeat the process for the middle and end of the story. **Beginning, middle, and end**
Thursday Set up a pretend campfire in your circle-time area. Announce a story problem that involves students around a campfire. Invite an appropriate number of students to act out the story problem to determine the answer. Continue until each student has had a turn to act out a problem. **Story problems**	Revisit the part of yesterday's story when George pours water on the camper's fire. Then have each student complete "Why Did That Happen?" (See directions on page 230.) **Cause and effect**
Friday On the board, draw a house and a tent. Ask students, "How is camping different from being at home?" Invite students to share their responses as you write them below the appropriate drawing. **Comparing**	**In My Bag** *(See directions on page 230.)*

Literacy and Math

Give each student ten small marshmallows. Announce a story problem, such as, "Jalen is roasting six marshmallows. His sister gives him two more. How many marshmallows does he have now?" Instruct each student to manipulate his marshmallows to find the answer. **Story problems**

Cut apart a copy of the short-vowel cards (page 231) and glue each card to a fish cutout (patterns on page 231). Attach a paper clip to each fish. Draw five frying pans on the board and label each with a different vowel. Have a student use a magnetic fishing pole to "catch" a fish, name the picture, and tape the fish to its pan. **Short vowels**

Write several random numbers on a board. Announce a number and then give a student a flashlight. Instruct the student to turn on the flashlight and point the beam at the stated number. **Number recognition**

Write a letter on each marshmallow cutout of a class supply and put the marshmallows in a disposable pie plate. Have the students sit in a circle and pass the plate. Each student takes a marshmallow and states the letter and a word that begins with the letter. Collect the marshmallows and repeat the activity. **Letter-sound associations**

Have each student glue five small marshmallow cutouts to a craft stick. Then have youngsters count the total number of marshmallows by fives as they join you one at a time around a pretend campfire. **Counting by fives**

Song

(sung to the tune of "Twinkle, Twinkle, Little Star")

We went camping one warm day.
Caught some fish along the way.
We put a tent up for the night
And slept beneath the stars so bright.
We made campfires and cooked too.
Camping is such fun to do.

Rhyming Words: Have students listen for and name the rhyming words in the song.

Journal Prompts

- Draw yourself and a friend camping. Write about what you would do.

- Write a response to the following question: "Would you like sleeping in a sleeping bag? Why or why not?" Illustrate your response.

- Draw yourself hiking. Write about the things you might see.

- Draw yourself eating your favorite camping food. Write about how you made the food.

- Write and complete the following sentence: "The best thing about camping is _____." Illustrate your sentence.

Instructions

Why Did That Happen?

Getting ready: Give each student a sheet of paper labeled as shown.

Steps:
1. On the side of the paper labeled "Cause," draw George pouring water on the camper's fire.
2. On the side of the paper labeled "Effect," draw what happened to George because he poured water on the camper's fire.
3. Turn your paper over and label the back side like the front.
4. Complete the back of your paper using the part of the story when George pulls the skunk's tail.

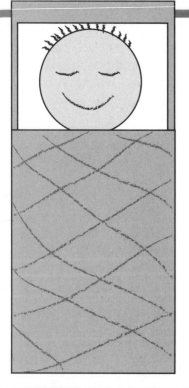

In My Bag

Materials for one sleeping bag: 8" colorful paper square cut as shown, 2 ½" x 3½" piece of white paper, 2½" skin-tone paper circle, crayons, glue

Steps:
1. Glue the white rectangle (pillow) beside the cut-out area of the square.
2. Draw a sleeping face on the circle and glue it on the pillow.
3. Fold the square in half so the pillow and head are visible. Unfold the square.
4. Spread glue on the section below the head and pillow. Then refold the square.
5. Decorate the sleeping bag if desired.

Short-Vowel Picture Cards and Fish Patterns

Use with the "Camping" unit on pages 227–230 and Monday's Group Time Activity on page 222.

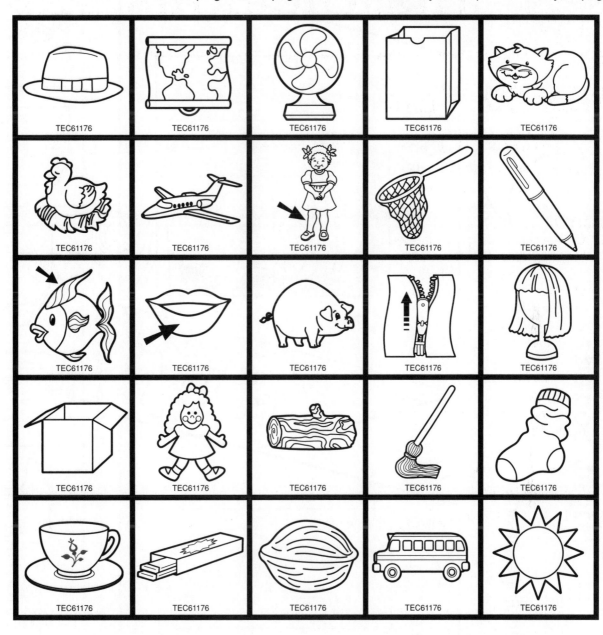

Day-by-Day Kindergarten Plans • ©The Mailbox® Books • TEC61176

Night Sounds

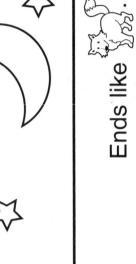

✂ Cut.

📎 Glue to match the ending sounds.

Ends like 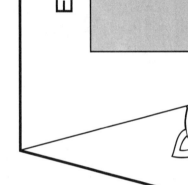 .

Ends like 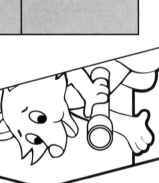 .

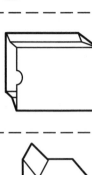

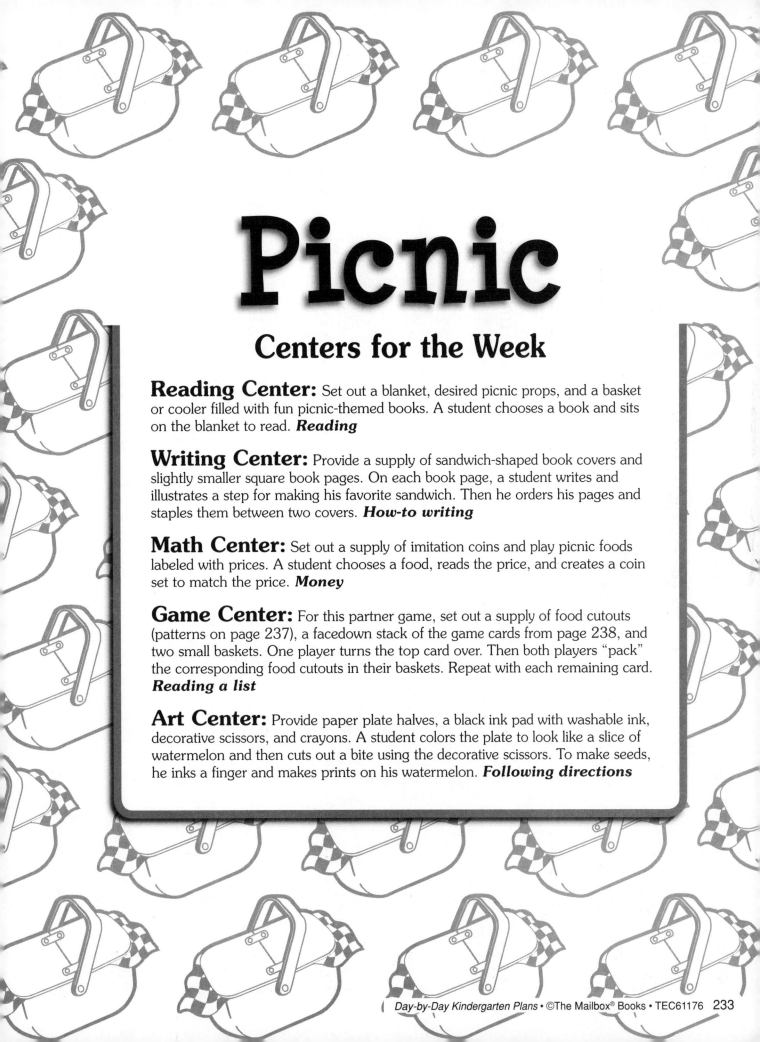

Picnic

Centers for the Week

Reading Center: Set out a blanket, desired picnic props, and a basket or cooler filled with fun picnic-themed books. A student chooses a book and sits on the blanket to read. ***Reading***

Writing Center: Provide a supply of sandwich-shaped book covers and slightly smaller square book pages. On each book page, a student writes and illustrates a step for making his favorite sandwich. Then he orders his pages and staples them between two covers. ***How-to writing***

Math Center: Set out a supply of imitation coins and play picnic foods labeled with prices. A student chooses a food, reads the price, and creates a coin set to match the price. ***Money***

Game Center: For this partner game, set out a supply of food cutouts (patterns on page 237), a facedown stack of the game cards from page 238, and two small baskets. One player turns the top card over. Then both players "pack" the corresponding food cutouts in their baskets. Repeat with each remaining card. ***Reading a list***

Art Center: Provide paper plate halves, a black ink pad with washable ink, decorative scissors, and crayons. A student colors the plate to look like a slice of watermelon and then cuts out a bite using the decorative scissors. To make seeds, he inks a finger and makes prints on his watermelon. ***Following directions***

Morning Group Time	Read-Alouds and Art

Monday

Ask youngsters to name activities that take place at picnics. Guide them to tell whether each activity takes closer to one minute or one hour to complete. Write students' responses on the board. ***Estimating time***

one minute	one hour
make a sandwich	make homemade lemonade
throw a football	drive to the picnic spot
eat a cookie	grill burgers

Draw a picnic basket on the board. Invite students to name food and nonfood items they would take on a picnic. Write student responses in the basket. Then read aloud *McDuff Saves the Day* by Rosemary Wells. ***Prior knowledge***

Tuesday

Write a high-frequency word on each of a class supply of paper plates. Have students sit in a circle, and give each student a plate. Have students pass the plates while you play a recording of music. After a few moments, stop the recording and ask a few students to read the word on the plates they're holding. Resume the music to play again. ***High-frequency words***

Revisit yesterday's story. Ask students to recall events in the story that might have led the author to title the book *McDuff Saves the Day*. ***Drawing conclusions***

Wednesday

Spread a large checkered tablecloth on the floor and have students sit in a circle around it. Begin passing a basket. When a child receives the basket, instruct him to pretend to put in the basket an object whose name begins with the letter *p* like *picnic*. Then invite him to recite and complete the following sentence: I'm packing my [object] for the picnic. ***Beginning sounds, oral language***

Read aloud *It's the Bear!* by Jez Alborough. Stop several times during the story and invite students to predict what will happen next. ***Making predictions***

Thursday

Give each student a card with a time written on it, repeating times as needed. Invite each child, in turn, to move the hands on a large clock manipulative to show the time on his card. Then have him say, "I am going on a picnic at [time]." ***Telling time***

2:00

Discuss the picnic locations in *It's the Bear!* and *McDuff Saves the Day*. Give each student a sheet of paper and have her draw a picture of a place she would like to go for a picnic and write about it. ***Setting, making connections***

Friday

Have each student complete "Picnic Snacks" on page 236. At a designated time, invite students to sit together outside and enjoy their snacks. ***Following written directions***

Picnic Snack Mix
3 scoops of pretzels
1 scoop of cereal puffs
2 scoops of cereal rings
1 scoop of mini cookies

Picnic Time
(See directions on page 236.)

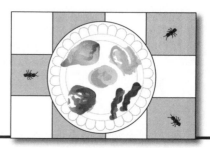

Literacy and Math

Give each student a copy of the basket pattern on page 238 and ten pieces of fruity cereal. Write a number word on the board. Instruct her to read the word and place the corresponding number of cereal pieces on the basket. **Reading number words**

five

Give each student in half the class a plastic fork and students in the other half plastic spoons. Instruct students to group themselves to make pairs containing one fork and one spoon. Then have the groups stand side by side with clearly defined space between them. Lead students in counting by twos. **Counting by twos**

On the board, draw and label a picnic food, such as an apple. Then ask a volunteer to draw a picture that shows more than one of the item. Label the picture with the plural form of the word. Repeat with other picnic items. Then have each student choose a picnic item, draw on a sheet of paper to show one and more than one, and label the pictures. **Plurals with s**

hot dog hot dogs

Give each student a napkin and ten small black pom-poms (ants). Announce a story problem, such as the following: Three ants are at a picnic; then four more join them. How many ants came to the picnic? Then have him manipulate the ants to solve the problem. Invite volunteers to share the solution to the problem. **Story problems**

Put assorted items—such as potato chip canisters, food boxes, and plastic oranges—in a picnic basket. Lay on the floor three plastic hoops labeled "cylinder," "rectangular prism," and "sphere." Invite a volunteer to remove an item from the basket and put it in the correct hoop. Continue as described for each remaining item. **Solid shapes**

Song

(sung to the tune of "Take Me Out to the Ballgame")

Let's all go on a picnic.
It's so much fun to do.
We'll pack some carrots and
    sandwiches,
And we'll take some of Mom's cookies
    too.
We'll open our picnic basket;
Spread blankets down on the ground.
Then we'll unpack all our food
And pass it around.

Punctuation: Display a copy of the song. Show students the apostrophe in the word *Let's* and discuss its purpose. Invite students to locate and circle the other apostrophes.

Journal Prompts

- Draw yourself packing a picnic basket. Write about the things you are putting in your basket.

- Draw yourself eating your favorite picnic food. Write about why it is your favorite.

- Draw a favorite picnic activity. Write about it.

- Write a response to the following question: If you could go on a picnic with anyone, who would it be? Illustrate your answer.

- Write a description of the perfect picnic location. Illustrate your description.

Instructions

Picnic Time

Materials for one project: six 4" white paper squares, 12" x 18" sheet of red construction paper, paper plate, sponges cut into the shapes of picnic foods, various colors of paint, glue, black marker

Steps:
1. To make a checkered picnic blanket, glue the white squares on the red paper as shown.
2. Create a plate of picnic food by dipping desired sponges in paint and making prints on the paper plate.
3. Glue the plate to the blanket.
4. Draw ants on the blanket.

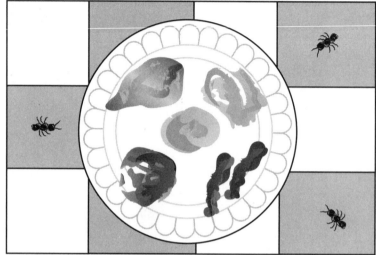

Picnic Snacks

Picnic Snack Mix

3 scoops of pretzels

1 scoop of cereal puffs

2 scoops of cereal rings

1 scoop of mini cookies

Getting ready: Set out labeled bowls containing cereals, mini cookies, and pretzels along with a scooper for each bowl. Post a simple snack mix recipe, like the one shown, and give each student a resealable plastic bag.

Steps:
1. Read the recipe and put the appropriate amount of each ingredient in your bag.
2. Seal your bag and shake it to mix the ingredients.

Chips

Juice

TEC61176

Game Cards and Basket Pattern

Use with the "Picnic" unit on pages 233–236.

2 sandwiches 3 apples 2 juice boxes TEC61176	3 oranges 2 apples 2 bags of chips TEC61176
4 sandwiches 3 bags of chips 1 orange TEC61176	1 sandwich 3 juice boxes 4 oranges TEC61176
2 apples 3 bags of chips 2 juice boxes TEC61176	3 sandwiches 2 apples 3 oranges TEC61176

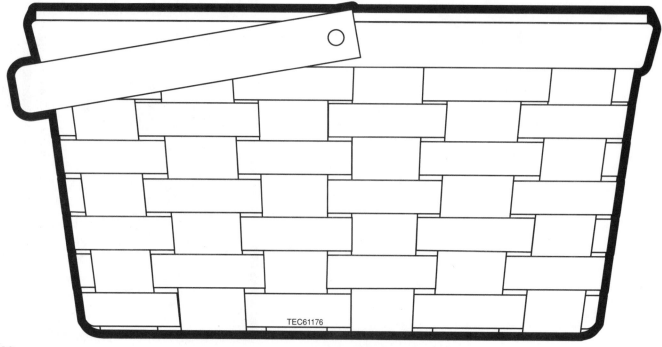

TEC61176

Day-by-Day Kindergarten Plans • ©The Mailbox® Books • TEC61176

Ice Cream

Centers for the Week

Reading Center: Write simple words on a supply of scoop cutouts and glue matching clip art on cone cutouts. (Cone and scoop patterns are on page 243.) A student reads the word on each scoop and then places it on top of the corresponding cone. *Matching words to pictures*

Writing Center: Provide blank paper and a supply of pencils, crayons, and markers. A student draws her favorite ice cream creation and writes how it tastes, looks, and feels. *Descriptive words*

Math Center: Set out a supersize banana split bowl cutout and a supply of different-colored ice cream scoop cutouts (patterns on page 243). A student places the scoops on the bowl to make a pattern. After copying the pattern onto a sheet of paper, he repeats the activity with a different pattern. *Patterning*

Art Center: Make a batch of puff paint (ice cream) by mixing together shaving cream, glue, and a small amount of paint. Set out the paint along with cone cutouts (pattern on page 243). A student glues a cone to a sheet of paper and then fingerpaints ice cream scoops above the cone. *Painting*

Game Center: For this partner game, provide two disposable bowls, an ice cream scooper, a supply of large pom-poms (ice cream scoops), and a facedown stack of number cards. In turn, each player takes a card and uses the scooper to put the corresponding number of scoops in her bowl. Next, the partners combine their scoops into one bowl and announce the sum. Then they empty the bowl and play another round. *Adding*

	Morning Group Time	Read-Alouds and Art
Monday	Program a class supply of scoop cutouts (pattern on page 243) with numbers up to 30. Give a scoop to each student and have her read the number. Announce a direction such as "If your number is less than 20, pretend to lick your ice cream scoop." Repeat using a different number each time. **Number sense**	Read aloud *From Cow to Ice Cream* by Bertram T. Knight. Then ask students to recall the steps of how ice cream is made through the sequence of photographs. **Sequence**
Tuesday	Give each student a cone cutout and six scoop cutouts: two brown, two pink, and two white (patterns on page 243). Have students pretend to be workers at an ice cream parlor. Then play the role of the customer as you order an ice cream treat, such as two scoops of vanilla, one scoop of chocolate, and one scoop of strawberry. Have each child make the described treat by stacking the appropriate scoops on the cone. **Following directions**	Revisit the pages from yesterday's book that show the various jobs in the ice cream industry. Discuss with students the different jobs and have them choose the job they think would be the best. Invite students to share their choices and the reasons for their choices. **Supporting an opinion**
Wednesday	Obtain ice cream in three unique flavors. List the flavors on the board and give students a sample of each flavor. Then have each student draw a tally mark beside the flavor he likes best. Lead students in counting and comparing the tally marks beside each flavor. **Tally marks**	Read aloud *Ice Cream Larry* by Daniel Pinkwater. Stop reading the story after Mr. Berg asks to speak with Larry. Invite students to predict what Mr. Berg wants to discuss with Larry. Then continue reading so students can check their predictions. **Making predictions**
Thursday	Post a large pink ice cream scoop cutout. Invite students to name real or made-up ice cream flavors that could be pink. List the flavors on the scoop. If desired, repeat the activity with different-colored scoops. **Critical thinking** strawberry bubble gum watermelon	Revisit the page in yesterday's story when Mr. Berg brings the Larry Bars to the hotel. Give each student a white paper rectangle and a craft stick. Have her design the wrapper for her own ice cream bar. **Responding to literature** 
Friday	Place a scoop of ice cream in a plastic bowl, another scoop in a glass bowl, and another in a metal pan. Place the three containers on a sunny windowsill. Ask students to predict which scoop will melt first and discuss their reasons. Periodically check the scoops until one melts completely. **Making predictions, observation**	**Scented Sundae** *(See directions on page 242.)* 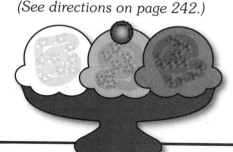

Literacy and Math

Label each of five white scoop cutouts with a different vowel and several brown scoops with consonants in chosen CVC words (pattern on page 243). Post a bowl cutout (pattern on page 243) and place the scoops nearby. Form words with the scoops and have students read them aloud. Then ask volunteers to use the scoops to form designated words. **CVC words**

Prepare a large paper sundae. Label each scoop with a different number. Place the sundae on the floor. Have a student toss two beanbags onto different numbers. Lead the class in announcing a corresponding addition sentence as you write it on the board. Then invite a volunteer to solve the problem. Repeat until each child has had a turn. **Adding**

Label three or four large bowl cutouts with rimes and post the bowls around the room. Write words that include the rimes on a class supply of scoop cutouts (pattern on page 243). Give each student a scoop and instruct her to read the word. Then have her walk to the correct bowl. After checking for accuracy, redistribute the scoops and repeat the activity. **Word families**

Have each student complete "Making Ice Cream" on page 242. Then have students help you write the steps for making ice cream so another class could follow them. **Sequencing steps**

Post a large ice cream cone cutout with ten scoop cutouts (patterns on page 243). Ask a volunteer to remove a scoop as you write the corresponding subtraction sentence on the board. Continue in this manner until all the scoops are gone. Then lead youngsters in discussing the resulting math pattern in the number sentences. **Subtraction**

Song

(sung to the tune of "When the Saints Go Marching In")

Ice cream is cold.
It's such a treat.
At anytime,
It's fun to eat.
Vanilla, chocolate, strawberry—
The taste of ice cream can't be beat.

Ending sounds: Display a copy of the song. Invite volunteers to locate and circle all the words that end with /t/. Discuss with students the sound at the end of each of the circled words.

Journal Prompts

- Draw yourself at an ice cream shop. Write about your picture.

- Write to complete the following sentence: "I like to eat ice cream _____." Illustrate your sentence.

- Draw yourself eating your favorite flavor of ice cream. Write about why it is your favorite.

- Write and complete the following sentence: "Ice cream is cold, and so is _____." Illustrate your sentence.

- Write and complete the following sentence: "The best thing about ice cream is _____." Illustrate your sentence.

Making Ice Cream

Materials for each child: small resealable plastic bag, large resealable plastic bag, ½ c. whole milk, 1 tsp. sugar, ¼ tsp. vanilla, 2 c. ice cubes, ½ c. table salt, plastic spoon

Steps:

1. Put milk, sugar, and vanilla in the small bag and seal it.
2. Put the ice and salt in the large bag. Then put the small bag in the large bag and seal it.
3. Shake the large bag until the mixture in the small bag thickens (approximately five minutes).
4. Open and discard the large bag. Then open the small bag and enjoy your ice cream.

Scented Sundae

Materials for one sundae: construction paper bowl (pattern on page 243), 3 construction paper scoops (1 white, 1 brown, and 1 pink), vanilla pudding mix, chocolate pudding mix, strawberry gelatin mix, red pom-pom, diluted glue, paintbrush, glue

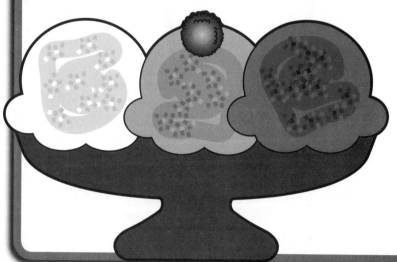

Steps:

1. Glue the scoops on the bowl.
2. Paint each scoop with the diluted glue.
3. Sprinkle the vanilla pudding mix on the white scoop, the strawberry gelatin mix on the pink scoop, and the chocolate pudding mix on the brown scoop.
4. Glue the red pom-pom to the top of the middle scoop.

TEC61176

TEC61176

TEC61176

Scoops to Share

Add.

5 + 0 = ___	3 + 4 = ___
6 + 2 = ___	3 + 3 = ___
4 + 6 = ___	7 + 2 = ___
7 + 0 = ___	5 + 3 = ___
4 + 5 = ___	2 + 8 = ___

's

Journal

_____'s

Journal

Day-by-Day Kindergarten Plans • ©The Mailbox® Books • TEC61176

_____'s

Journal

_____'s

Journal

What's New?

Teacher: _____

Date: _____

What We're Learning

Reminders

Help Wanted

Looking Ahead

Announcements

What's New?

Teacher: _____

Date: _____

What We're Learning

Reminders

Help Wanted

Looking Ahead

Announcements

What's New?

Teacher: _____

Date: _____

What We're Learning

Reminders

Help Wanted

Announcements

Looking Ahead

What's New?

Teacher: _____

Date: _____

What We're Learning

Reminders

Help Wanted

Looking Ahead

Announcements

Day-by-Day Kindergarten Plans • ©The Mailbox® Books • TEC61176

Note

A Note From School

A Note From School

Note

A Note From School

Note

Note

A Note From School